Kotlin Quick Start Guide

Core features to get you ready for developing applications

Marko Devcic

BIRMINGHAM - MUMBAI

Kotlin Quick Start Guide

Commissioning Editor: Richa Tripathi
Acquisition Editor: Siddharth Mandal
Content Development Editor: Kirk Dsouza
Technical Editor: Shweta Jadhav
Copy Editor: Safis Editing
Project Coordinator: Hardik Bhinde
Proofreader: Safis Editing
Indexer: Mariammal Chettiyar
Graphics: Jason Monteiro
Production Coordinator: Deepika Naik

First published: August 2018

Production reference: 1300818

Published by Packt Publishing Ltd.
Livery Place
35 Livery Street
Birmingham
B3 2PB, UK.

ISBN 978-1-78934-418-9

www.packtpub.com

This book is dedicated to my son, Bruno.

– Marko Devcic

`mapt.io`

Mapt is an online digital library that gives you full access to over 5,000 books and videos, as well as industry leading tools to help you plan your personal development and advance your career. For more information, please visit our website.

Why subscribe?

- Spend less time learning and more time coding with practical eBooks and Videos from over 4,000 industry professionals

- Improve your learning with Skill Plans built especially for you

- Get a free eBook or video every month

- Mapt is fully searchable

- Copy and paste, print, and bookmark content

PacktPub.com

Did you know that Packt offers eBook versions of every book published, with PDF and ePub files available? You can upgrade to the eBook version at `www.PacktPub.com` and as a print book customer, you are entitled to a discount on the eBook copy. Get in touch with us at `service@packtpub.com` for more details.

At `www.PacktPub.com`, you can also read a collection of free technical articles, sign up for a range of free newsletters, and receive exclusive discounts and offers on Packt books and eBooks.

Contributors

About the author

Marko Devcic is a software engineer currently working as an Android developer for an Austrian company called mySugr in Vienna. He has a master's degree in engineering from the University of Zagreb in Croatia. Over the years, he has worked with various technologies and languages, mostly C#, Java, and Kotlin.

He is passionate about technology and software development. He loves reading about programming languages.

In his spare time, he writes codes and contributes towards open source projects. You can follow him on GitHub (username `deva666`). He also likes to write about Kotlin, C#, and programming in general on his web page. When he is not behind a computer, he's practicing Brazilian Jiu-Jitsu or spending time with his son.

About the reviewer

Mitchell Wong Ho was born in Johannesburg, South Africa, where he completed his national diploma in electrical engineering. Mitchell's software career development started on embedded systems and then moved to Microsoft desktop/server applications. Mitchell has been programming in Java since 2000 on J2ME, JEE, desktop, and Android applications, and has more recently been advocating Kotlin for Android. Mitchell made a significant contribution to the development of the *Kotlin Programming Cookbook*, which was published recently by Packt.

Packt is searching for authors like you

If you're interested in becoming an author for Packt, please visit `authors.packtpub.com` and apply today. We have worked with thousands of developers and tech professionals, just like you, to help them share their insight with the global tech community. You can make a general application, apply for a specific hot topic that we are recruiting an author for, or submit your own idea.

Table of Contents

Preface

Kotlin is a relatively new language that is gaining popularity rapidly, thanks to its numerous unique features that increase developer productivity. It is primarily used for mobile (Android) and server-side (backend) development but can be used anywhere Java is used. Thanks to its other compiler, which transforms it into JavaScript, it can even be used for frontend web development. This book targets newcomers to the language and tries to bring them to intermediate-advanced levels of Kotlin knowledge.

Who this book is for

This book covers the basic features of the language and its syntax, so no prior knowledge of Kotlin is required. You should have at least basic knowledge of general programming. You should know what control-flow statements, variables, classes, and basic data structures are.

What this book covers

Chapter 1, *Introducing Kotlin*, covers general features of the language and shows the reader how to install an IDE and the Kotlin compiler.

Chapter 2, *Kotlin Basics*, introduces the reader to the language syntax and explores the basic building blocks of the language: functions, variables, basic types, and so on.

Chapter 3, *Classes and Object-Oriented Programming*, focuses on the object-oriented features of the language. The chapter explores classes and interfaces and how they are extended and implemented. The chapter also shows some features that are specific to Kotlin, such as objects, companion objects, and sealed classes.

Chapter 4, *Functions and Lambdas*, shows how functions are first-class citizens in Kotlin. The chapter also shows Kotlin function features that are not present in Java, such as default argument values, named parameters, and function inlining.

Chapter 5, *Advanced Kotlin*, deals with more advanced features of Kotlin, such as operator overloading, generics, receiver functions, and constructs for multi-threaded programming.

Chapter 6, *Kotlin Standard Library*, shows some really useful functions that ship with Kotlin and also explores the Collections API.

Chapter 7, *Coding a Dictionary App with Kotlin*, is the chapter where we put Kotlin into practice. We summarize our learning from previous chapters and build a desktop dictionary application.

To get the most out of this book

Since Kotlin compiles to Java bytecode and uses Java's types and build tools (Maven and Gradle), readers with a Java background will probably find Kotlin a bit easier than those without. But a Java background is not a requirement, as this book is intended for readers who are completely new to Kotlin/Java and the JVM ecosystem.

This book doesn't teach programming, so readers that have knowledge of any modern general-purpose programming language will find content in this book more understandable than those who don't.

Download the example code files

You can download the example code files for this book from your account at www.packtpub.com. If you purchased this book elsewhere, you can visit www.packtpub.com/support and register to have the files emailed directly to you.

You can download the code files by following these steps:

1. Log in or register at www.packtpub.com.
2. Select the **SUPPORT** tab.
3. Click on **Code Downloads & Errata**.
4. Enter the name of the book in the **Search** box and follow the onscreen instructions.

Once the file is downloaded, please make sure that you unzip or extract the folder using the latest version of:

- WinRAR/7-Zip for Windows
- Zipeg/iZip/UnRarX for Mac
- 7-Zip/PeaZip for Linux

The code bundle for the book is also hosted on GitHub at https://github.com/PacktPublishing/Kotlin-Quick-Start-Guide. In case there's an update to the code, it will be updated on the existing GitHub repository.

We also have other code bundles from our rich catalog of books and videos available at `https://github.com/PacktPublishing/`. Check them out!

Download the color images

We also provide a PDF file that has color images of the screenshots/diagrams used in this book. You can download it here: `http://www.packtpub.com/sites/default/files/downloads/KotlinQuickStartGuide_ColorImages.pdf`.

Conventions used

There are a number of text conventions used throughout this book.

`CodeInText`: Indicates code words in text, database table names, folder names, filenames, file extensions, pathnames, dummy URLs, user input, and Twitter handles. Here is an example: "Mount the downloaded `WebStorm-10*.dmg` disk image file as another disk in your system."

A block of code is set as follows:

```
<plugin>
    <artifactId>kotlin-maven-plugin</artifactId>
    <groupId>org.jetbrains.kotlin</groupId>
    <version>${kotlin.version}</version>
    <configuration>
        <jvmTarget>1.8</jvmTarget>
    </configuration>
</plugin>
```

Bold: Indicates a new term, an important word, or words that you see onscreen. For example, words in menus or dialog boxes appear in the text like this. Here is an example: "Select **System info** from the **Administration** panel."

Warnings or important notes appear like this.

Tips and tricks appear like this.

Get in touch

Feedback from our readers is always welcome.

General feedback: Email `feedback@packtpub.com` and mention the book title in the subject of your message. If you have questions about any aspect of this book, please email us at `questions@packtpub.com`.

Errata: Although we have taken every care to ensure the accuracy of our content, mistakes do happen. If you have found a mistake in this book, we would be grateful if you would report this to us. Please visit `www.packtpub.com/submit-errata`, selecting your book, clicking on the Errata Submission Form link, and entering the details.

Piracy: If you come across any illegal copies of our works in any form on the Internet, we would be grateful if you would provide us with the location address or website name. Please contact us at `copyright@packtpub.com` with a link to the material.

If you are interested in becoming an author: If there is a topic that you have expertise in and you are interested in either writing or contributing to a book, please visit `authors.packtpub.com`.

Reviews

Please leave a review. Once you have read and used this book, why not leave a review on the site that you purchased it from? Potential readers can then see and use your unbiased opinion to make purchase decisions, we at Packt can understand what you think about our products, and our authors can see your feedback on their book. Thank you!

For more information about Packt, please visit `packtpub.com`.

Introducing Kotlin

Kotlin is a relatively new programming language, developed by JetBrains, the company that stands behind some of the most popular developer IDEs and tools, such as IntelliJ IDEA and ReSharper. JetBrains didn't create Kotlin so that they could make money on it; instead, they started the project because they wanted to solve their own development problems. In 2010, when the project started, Java was the dominant language in their code base. However, the development team wasn't happy with Java and some of its old-fashioned features. They looked for more modern alternatives to Java, but couldn't find one that satisfied their requirements in the existing JVM languages. Scala was popular at the time and was considered, but it had issues such as slow compile times.

So, they decided to create a completely new language by themselves. Since they already had a huge code base written in Java, rewriting everything in this new language wouldn't have been practical. So, Java interoperability was one of the top priorities.

Preview of the language was released in 2011 and the developer community reacted positively to it. Since then, the popularity of the language has grown rapidly. The language is open source and JetBrains' developers are not the only ones working on it. The project (language, compiler, standard library, tools, and so on) is hosted on GitHub and developers all around the world are contributing to it. Currently, there around 200 contributors to the Kotlin repository. Developers are also adopting it and more and more companies are using it in their production code. Even big companies, such as Atlassian, Square, Uber, and Pinterest, use Kotlin in production. Google also supports Kotlin development. It made Kotlin an officially supported language for building Android apps.

Now that we know how Kotlin started – and that its main goals are great Java interoperability and, at the same time, better productivity than Java – we can say that Kotlin is a general purpose, statically typed, object-oriented and functional programming language, that (primarily) targets JVM. The name Kotlin comes from an island near St.Petersburg, just as Java was named after an island in Indonesia.

In this chapter we will focus on:

- Compiling and running Kotlin
- Kotlin's uses
- Java interoperability
- Build tools
- Setting up the development environment

Compiling and running Kotlin

Kotlin started as a JVM language, so the first compiler for Kotlin was targeting Java bytecode. But now, there are also compilers that can turn Kotlin into JavaScript and one that is still experimental, that produces native code.

Thanks to this compiler and the native code output, soon it will be possible to write apps with Kotlin that don't require additional runtimes.

This book will focus on Kotlin running on JVM, as this is the most popular usage of Kotlin today. But most of the things learned here can also be applied to other Kotlin platforms (both JavaScript and Native).

Kotlin source code is stored in files with a .kt extension, similar to the way that Java's are stored with a .java extension. Compiling Kotlin .kt files produces .class files that contain Java bytecode.

These are the same .class files that a Java compiler produces.

From there, .class files are bundled inside .jar files to form a module (a library or an app).

Since JVM only knows about Java bytecode, running apps written in Kotlin is no different from how they are written in Java.

One additional step is needed to run Kotlin modules or apps. Kotlin has its own standard library, which builds upon Java's Standard Library, and it has to be distributed with your module or app. Luckily, the Kotlin compiler does this step for us (if you are using the compiler from the command-line, just add the -include-runtime argument to a kotlinc command). Also, with the size of around 800 KB, we can say that the Kotlin standard library is relatively small and you shouldn't be worried about it.

The following diagram shows how Kotlin source code is compiled and run on the JVM:

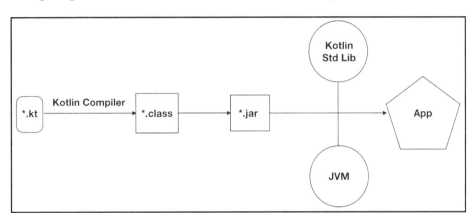

Kotlin's uses

Now that we know that Kotlin apps run on the JVM, we also know that it basically means that Kotlin can be used for anything that Java could be used for.

Today, Java is really popular for backend (server) development and Kotlin can be used for any kind of server development. Whether it is web apps that serve HTML content, a backend for REST APIs or Microservices, Kotlin can do the job. Not only that, thanks to the Kotlin JavaScript compiler, it can also be used for building frontend web Apps. So it is entirely possible to create a web App (both backend and frontend) using only one language.

Another area where Java used to be dominant was in native Android development (other JVM languages could also be used, but none has really gained popularity on Android). This is where Kotlin has probably gained the most popularity. In one part, due to Google officially supporting it for Android development, and, secondly, because Android is still stuck on Java 6. Kotlin, with its modern features, spread rapidly among the Android developers' community.

Kotlin can also be used for developing desktop apps since both JavaFX and Swing UI libraries can be called from Kotlin.

Java interoperability

As mentioned before, Java interoperability was one of the main goals during the development of Kotlin and it is implemented seamlessly. You can call from Kotlin existing libraries compiled with Java; you can also extend a class written in Java or implement an interface written in Java and use all its types from the Java Standard Library.

But the best part is that you can have Kotlin side-by-side with the existing Java code. There's nothing preventing you from writing half of your project in Java and the other half in Kotlin.

IDEs (IntelliJ or Eclipse with a Kotlin plugin) support navigating in both Kotlin and Java files in the same project. Also, debugging and stepping through code from a project with both languages is not a problem at all. Refactoring Kotlin or Java code will also correctly update the references in another language as well.

This interoperability is also visible in the Kotlin Standard Library. Standard Library relies heavily on Java Standard Library and extends a lot of types from it. For example, Kotlin doesn't have it's own collections classes, it uses ones from Java. Java library has been battle tested and so it wouldn't make sense to reinvent the wheel.

Java-Kotlin interoperability also works in another direction. You can call functions written in Kotlin from Java, extend types and implement interfaces declared in Kotlin.

Build tools

For anything more than a simple app, you will probably use some kind of build automation tools like Maven, Ant or Gradle. The good news is that Kotlin is supported by all three of them.

In this section, will see how to set up Maven and Gradle tools for development with Kotlin.

If you are starting a new project with Gradle or Maven, your IDE probably can generate the required files for you. Here you will learn how to add Kotlin manually because you might have an existing Java project and want to start using Kotlin with it or in case you don't want to use an IDE.

Gradle

In your Gradle project, you have the `build.gradle` file located somewhere in the root of your project. Make sure that you have this `buildScript` section in that file.

```
buildscript {
    ext.kotlin_version = '1.2.40'

    repositories {
        mavenCentral()
    }
    dependencies {
        classpath "org.jetbrains.kotlin:kotlin-gradle-
plugin:$kotlin_version"
    }
}
```

This tells Gradle to use a Kotlin plugin and adds Maven central to the list of repositories. With the plugin added, we still need the Kotlin standard library to be able to compile a Kotlin source code. If you have multiple Gradle modules, make sure that the module's `build.gradle` file in which you plan to use Kotlin has the following:

```
apply plugin: "kotlin"

repositories {
    mavenCentral()
}

dependencies {
    compile "org.jetbrains.kotlin:kotlin-stdlib:$kotlin_version"
}

compileKotlin {
    kotlinOptions.jvmTarget = "1.8"
}
```

If you don't have multiple `build.gradle` files, then put this to the root `build.gradle` file. The same one in which you added the Kotlin plugin.

You can also set various compiler options under the compile Kotlin section. For example, with the `kotlinOptions.jvmTarget = "1.8"` option we told the Kotlin compiler to produce Java 1.8 compatible bytecode.

Now, if you sync your Gradle project, you should be able to add Kotlin files to it and compile them with Gradle.

Maven

If Maven is your build tool of choice, then setting up Kotlin will be just as easy.

In the same way as with Gradle, we first need to add a Kotlin plugin to a `pom.xml` file. You can do this by adding these lines to the plugins section:

```
<plugin>
    <artifactId>kotlin-maven-plugin</artifactId>
    <groupId>org.jetbrains.kotlin</groupId>
    <version>${kotlin.version}</version>
    <executions>
        <execution>
            <id>compile</id>
            <goals><goal>compile</goal></goals>
        </execution>
    </executions>
</plugin>
```

We can define a Kotlin version at one place, inside the properties section:

```
<properties>
    <kotlin.version>1.2.40</kotlin.version>
</properties>
```

In the same way as with Gradle, the Kotlin standard library needs to be added to `dependencies`.

```
<dependencies>
    <dependency>
        <groupId>org.jetbrains.kotlin</groupId>
        <artifactId>kotlin-stdlib</artifactId>
        <version>${kotlin.version}</version>
    </dependency>
</dependencies>
```

If you are targeting JDK 8, you can replace `kotlin-stdlib` with `kotlin-stdlib-jdk8` so you can have Kotlin extension functions that cover the latest APIs from JDK 8.

This should be enough if you plan on only writing Kotlin. If you are mixing Kotlin and Java inside a Maven project, a Kotlin compiler needs to run before a Java compiler. To instruct Maven to compile Kotlin first, the Kotlin plugin needs to be before the Maven compiler plugin.

Here's what the complete build section looks like:

```xml
<build>
    <plugins>
        <plugin>
            <artifactId>kotlin-maven-plugin</artifactId>
            <groupId>org.jetbrains.kotlin</groupId>
            <version>${kotlin.version}</version>
            <executions>
                <execution>
                    <id>compile</id>
                    <goals> <goal>compile</goal> </goals>
                    <configuration>
                        <sourceDirs>
<sourceDir>${project.basedir}/src/main/kotlin</sourceDir>
<sourceDir>${project.basedir}/src/main/java</sourceDir>
                        </sourceDirs>
                    </configuration>
                </execution>
            </executions>
        </plugin>
        <plugin>
            <groupId>org.apache.maven.plugins</groupId>
            <artifactId>maven-compiler-plugin</artifactId>
            <version>3.5.1</version>
            <executions>
                <execution>
                    <id>default-compile</id>
                    <phase>none</phase>
                </execution>
                <execution>
                    <id>java-compile</id>
                    <phase>compile</phase>
                    <goals> <goal>compile</goal> </goals>
                </execution>
            </executions>
        </plugin>
    </plugins>
</build>
```

Finally, there are various Kotlin compiler options that can be set under the configuration section of a Kotlin plugin. Here's an example of how to instruct the compiler to produce a Java 1.8 compatible bytecode.

```
<plugin>
    <artifactId>kotlin-maven-plugin</artifactId>
    <groupId>org.jetbrains.kotlin</groupId>
    <version>${kotlin.version}</version>
    <configuration>
        <jvmTarget>1.8</jvmTarget>
    </configuration>
</plugin>
```

Setting up the development environment

Although you could use a basic text editor for writing Kotlin source code and compile it using the command-line tools, you will make your life easier if you use an IDE for coding. IDE can provide code completion, syntax highlighting, stepping through code while debugging, refactoring, and more.

IntelliJ IDEA is probably the most popular IDE for Java today. The IDE comes from the same company that created Kotlin and, of course, Kotlin is a first class citizen inside IntelliJ. This book uses IntelliJ, and it is recommended that you use it as well. But other popular IDEs for Java could also work, such as Eclipse or NetBeans (a Kotlin plugin would be needed). The great thing about IntelliJ is that the latest versions already come with a Kotlin plugin pre-installed, so the IDE is ready for Kotin development out of the box. This plugin already has a Kotlin compiler and also enables Kotlin syntax highlighting inside the code editor.

Another benefit of using IntelliJ is that it comes with a Java to Kotlin converter. If you have some Java code, or you are working in a mixed (both Java and Kotlin) project, you can convert Java code to Kotlin with the click of a button. Some minor changes might be needed in the resulting Kotlin code but in general, this converter works reasonably well.

IntelliJ has a paid for Ultimate version and a free Community version. The Express version has everything needed for Kotlin development and can be downloaded from the JetBrains website https://www.jetbrains.com/idea/download/. It's available for all platforms (Mac, Linux, and Windows).

Finally, if you are just trying out the syntax or just getting a feel for the language, there is a free online compiler and IDE available at `https://try.kotlinlang.org/`.

What's great about this online IDE is that it has plenty of examples of Kotlin features. There is also a section called Koans which has smaller code problems with the goal of teaching Kotlin. So, it might be worth checking it out.

Now that we have an IDE installed, let's get the first taste of Kotlin. Inside Intellij, start a new project and select Kotlin from the bar on the left and then select the **Kotlin/JVM** option, as seen in the following screenshot:

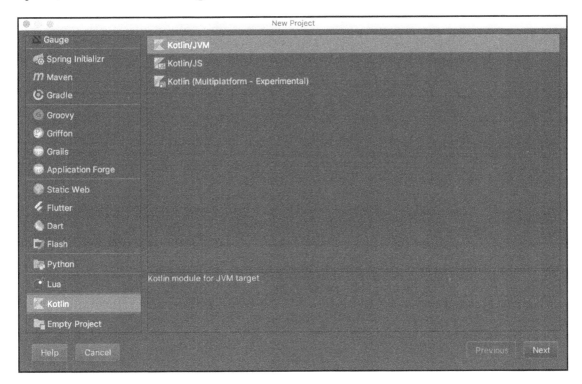

On the next screen, enter your project name and select **KotlinJavaRuntime** in the **Use library** section.

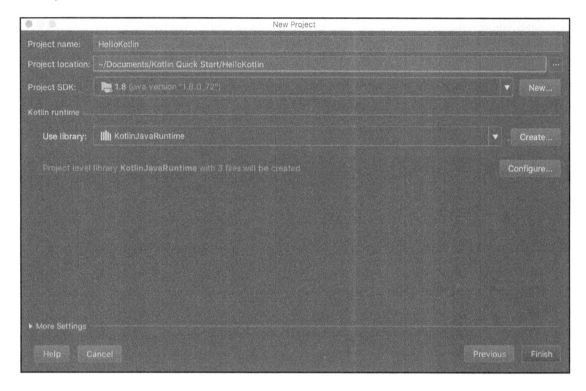

This will be enough to compile and run Kotlin code from the IDE. For smaller examples, setting up Maven or Gradle would be an overkill.

Now that we have a Kotlin project, let's add some Kotlin code: the standard Hello World printed to the console. Add a file named `Main.kt` inside the `src` folder.

Inside that file add the following code:

```
fun main(args: Array<String>) {
    println("Hello World!")
}
```

Now, there should be a little green icon in the gutter of the text editor and if you click it you should see "Hello World!" in the output.

Summary

In this chapter, we took a look at the history of Kotlin and explained how it compiles to Java bytecode. Thanks to Kotlin's great interoperability with Java, we've seen that it has wide use cases, from Backend apps to Mobile and Desktop apps. We'll be using IntelliJ IDEA as our IDE in this book, as Kotlin is supported out of the box. Finally, we discussed build tools that support Kotlin.

In the next chapter, we'll start with exploring the language and learning the basics.

2
Kotlin Basics

With Kotlin IDE installed, it is now time to start learning the basic elements of the language. In this chapter, you can learn about local variables and functions and basic Kotlin Types. If you are a Java programmer, in this chapter you'll see what sets Kotlin apart from Java. You'll see how type inference works and how Kotlin, with its support for Nullable Types, tries to prevent `NullPointerExceptions`.

Here is the complete overview of topics you will learn in this chapter:

- Functions
- Local variables
- Local functions
- Type inference
- Basic types
- Nullable types
- Casting
- Control flow
- Exceptions
- Packages
- Visibility modifiers

Functions

Functions in Kotlin are declared with the `fun` keyword. Following the keyword comes the function name, then parentheses, which contain optional function parameters. In Kotlin, return type comes at the end of the function definition, after a colon.

Here's a function in Kotlin that adds two numbers and returns the result:

```
fun add(a: Int, b: Int): Int {
    val result: Int = a + b
    return result
}
```

This function accepts two parameters of type Int (32-bit integer), has a local variable of type Int, and also returns an Int.

If you are familiar with Java, you might have noticed that types of parameters and local variables come after their name. In Java their type declaration comes first.

Calling this function would look like this:

```
val result: Int = add(1, 1)
```

In Java, every declaration, such as a field or a function, has to be inside a class. Kotlin doesn't have such restrictions and will allow you to declare functions on a file level, outside of a class. To make it compatible with Java bytecode, a Kotlin compiler will generate a class for your file-level declarations and declare them as static members of that class.

The name of the generated class is the name of the containing file, plus the Kt suffix.

The file named `FileDeclaration.kt` is declared in the following command:

```
fun fileLevelFunctions() {
    println("I'm declared without a class")
}
```

If you were to call this file-level function from Java, you would need to access it as a static member of a class that a Kotlin compiler generated. This can be seen in the following command:

```
public class JavaClass {
    public void foo() {
        FileDeclarationKt.fileLevelFunction();
    }
}
```

Kotlin also supports writing functions with expression body. In the first example, function add has a block body. Block body is everything inside the curly braces. That function can be simplified because the local variable is redundant. So, we could have written it as return a + b. In that case, we can write add function with an expression body like this:

```
fun addAsExpression(a: Int, b: Int): Int = a + b
```

You can see that the curly braces and the return keyword are dropped.

If you have a function that doesn't return a result (`void` function), in Kotlin you can declare it as Unit returning or omit the return type completely. The following command shows this:

```
fun printToConsole(input: String): Unit {
    println(input)
}
```

No return type is also allowed and is equal to the preceding command:

```
fun printToConsole2(input: String) {
    println(input)
}
```

Have you noticed that we haven't used semicolons for marking an end of a line as we would have to in Java? Semicolons are optional in Kotlin, the compiler can figure out where the line ends. In fact, you'll get a compiler warning if you place a semicolon at the end of a line.

Local variables

Local variables can be declared in two ways: first, with the `val` keyword, then they are immutable (the variable cannot be reassigned). If you are coming from Java, `val` would be equal to variables declared with a `final` keyword.

Secondly, you can declare a local variable with a `var` keyword; then it is considered mutable and the value can be reassigned after a declaration.

The following command demonstrates that it will not compile, because the `bar` local variable cannot be reassigned:

```
fun immutable() {
    val bar: String = "Kotlin"
    bar = "Kotlin is awesome" // compiler error
}
```

And, when declared with `var`, the compiler allows a local variable to be reassigned:

```
fun mutable() {
    var bar: String = "Kotlin"
    bar = "Kotlin is awesome"
}
```

You should favor immutable variables. The compiler will give you a warning if you use a mutable variable but only assign it once.

Whether you declare a variable as mutable or immutable, it has to have a value when it is declared, or, if it doesn't have a value, the compiler must be sure that the variable is properly initialized in the scope. This example will compile because the compiler knows that the variable is initialized and has not been used before initialization:

```
val bar: String
if (true) {
    bar = "Foo"
}
else {
    bar = "Bar"
}
```

Local functions

Local functions are functions declared inside a function. They are also called nested functions. They are popular in scripting languages, but some other modern Object-Oriented languages, like Scala, Swift, and C# (since 7.0) also have them. One of the uses of local functions is code reuse. You can extract a piece of code that is repeated inside a local function so the code can be reused:

```
fun printUserDetails(user: User) {
    fun tryPrint(str: String) {
        if (str.length > 5) {
            println(str)
        }
        else {
            println("I print strings with more than 5 characters")
        }
    }
    tryPrint(user.firstName)
    tryPrint(user.lastName)
    tryPrint(user.address)
}
```

You can see how the function `tryPrint` is declared inside the `printUserDetails` function. We can call the nested function just as we would a normal function. The only difference between this and regular functions is the visibility. Local functions are only visible inside the function they were declared in. You cannot call a local function from a function that doesn't contain it.

Type inference

Declaring types in Kotlin is optional. This is a feature of a Kotlin compiler called Type inference. The compiler can infer the type from the context of the usage. Kotlin is a strongly and statically typed language, so omitting types doesn't mean that you lose type safety.

Here's an example of type inference:

```
val str = "Kotlin"
```

`str` variable is of type String and the compiler knows this from the String literal that is initializing the variable. That's why, if you try to assign a different type to this variable, you'll get a compiler error, as can be seen in the following:

```
var str = "Kotlin"
str = 1 // compiler error
```

Type inference doesn't just work on local variables, but also on functions with expression bodies, generic types, closures and lambdas. You'll see more type inference in practice in following chapters.

Basic types

If you are familiar with Java, then you probably know that Java has primitive (value) types and reference types.

The differences between them are that primitive type variables store the actual value of the type in their memory location (usually on the Stack) and reference type variables store the reference (memory address) to another memory location (on the Heap) where the actual data is stored.

Primitive types in Java also have their **Boxed** (Boxing is an automatic conversion of a primitive type to a reference type) version, a reference type. For example, a primitive `int` (32-bit integer) has a reference type in type `Integer`.

Kotlin doesn't have this distinction between primitive and reference type. This doesn't mean a Kotlin compiler cannot emit primitive types in Java bytecode. In fact, it would be really inefficient if Kotlin had only reference types.

Kotlin only hides this distinction from a developer. The compiler emits Java bytecode according to usage. In most cases, it will emit primitive types in Java bytecode, except when the variable is declared as nullable (remember that primitive type variables hold their value, null can be assigned only to reference types), or when its type is a generic parameter (you'll learn about generics and type erasure in following chapters).

Numbers

Numbers in Kotlin can be represented with integer types and floating point number types. Integer types are `Byte`, `Short`, `Int`, and `Long`.

Floating point number types are `Float`, and `Double`.

The following table shows all the number types with their memory sizes and default values:

Type	Size	Default Value
Byte	8 bit	0
Short	16 bit	0
Int	32 bit	0
Long	64 bit	0L
Float	32 bit	0.0F
Double	64 bit	0.0D

The following example shows how to initialize number types with literals:

```
val long: Long = 9999L

val int: Int = 999

val short: Short = 99

val byte: Byte = 9


val float: Float = 9.99F

val double: Double = 9.99999
```

Kotlin also allows the use of hexadecimal and binary numbers in literals:

```
val hex: Int = 0XFF

val binary:Int = 0b1001001
```

All number types have extension functions in the Kotlin standard library for converting to other number types. Here's how you can convert an Int type to all other number types:

```
val int = 1
val float = int.toFloat()
val double = int.toDouble()
val long = int.toLong()
val byte = int.toByte()
val short = int.toShort()
```

Boolean

The `boolean` data type is no different from other languages. It can have two values, `true` or `false`:

```
val booleanTrue: Boolean = true

val booleanFalse: Boolean = false
```

You can also initialize a boolean variable with an expression which evaluates to true or false, as this example shows:

```
val booleanTrue: Boolean = 1 < 100
```

Characters

Characters in Kotlin are represented with `Char` type. The character literal is declared with a single quote:

```
val a: Char = 'a'
```

There are not many differences from Java's `char` type, except that the Kotlin Standard Library adds several extension methods that make working with the `Char` type easier. For example, you can get a number type representation of a char with these functions. Here's how you'd get an `Int` value from a `Char`:

```
val num: Int = 'a'.toInt()
```

Strings

Kotlin, like most other modern languages (Java included), has immutable strings. The same `String` class from Java is used in Kotlin, but Kotlin has quite a lot of extension methods in the standard library that add additional functionality to it.

But, there is one big difference from Java: equality comparison. Kotlin overrides the `==` operator so it can be used to compare Strings based on their value, not their reference (memory address). In Java, if you want to check if Strings are equal based on their value, you have to compare them with an equals method.

String variables are usually declared with `String` literals, which have to be enclosed in double quotes, as the following command shows:

```
val s: String = "Kotlin"
```

Another great thing with Strings in Kotlin is that String templating is supported. This means that you can insert variables or expressions inside String literals. In Java, you would have to concatenate Strings with the + operator, but in Kotlin you can create a String like this:

```
fun printPersonDetails(person: Person)
{
    println("${person.name} was born in ${person.birthYear} year")
}
```

If a Person object is passed to this function with properties `name` = `John` and `birthYear` = `1990`, this will print **John was born in 1990 year**.

Finally, Kotlin supports raw String literals. They are declared with triple quotes and they have no escaping. A multiline raw String literal would be declared like this:

```
val multiLine: String = """
Hello Kotlin!
Nice to meet you!
"""
```

Base type

Although Kotlin builds upon Java's type system, not all the types are the same in Kotlin. One of these differences is the base type. Java has the `Object` class from which all reference types implicitly inherit. Kotlin's base type is called `Any` and it is similar to `Object`. `Any` has only three methods from the `Object`: `hashcode`, `equals` and `toString`.

Arrays

Arrays in Kotlin are not part of the language as they are in Java. In Kotlin, they are generic collection types. We'll cover generics in later chapters. For now, we can describe them as types that have other types as a parameter. For example, this is how a Strings array is declared in Kotlin:

```
Array<String>
```

Kotlin also has specific array types for each of the Java primitive types. The reason for this is that only reference types can be generic type parameters and primitives would be automatically boxed (wrapped into reference types). There is the `IntArray` class, `CharArray`, `LongArray` and so on, for each primitive type.

The easiest way to create an array is to use the `arrayOf` function from the standard library, whether it is a primitive or a reference type. An array will then be initialized with the arguments you have passed to this function:

```
val intArray = arrayOf(1, 2, 3)
```

You can also create arrays for use with the constructor of each class. The constructor accepts two parameters, size of the array, and a function that will initialize the array by calling this function for each element. Here's how you would initialize an array which holds squares of numbers 1 to 10:

```
val squares = IntArray(10, { i -> (i + 1) * (i + 1) })
```

Nullable types

When you want to state that a reference type doesn't point to a memory address, you can assign it a null value. If you have ever used Java, you probably experienced the `NullPointerException` fail, as it is one of the most common errors. This error is raised by the runtime when you dereference a null variable.

This decision, to have nulls in Java, is criticized a lot and is also sometimes called a *Billion Dollar mistake*. The introduction of the optional type in Java 8, tries to address this problem.

Kotlin tries to prevent these mistakes with supporting nullability in its type system. With nullable types, Kotlin tries to prevent null pointer errors during compilation and reduce the possibility of null pointer errors during runtime.

All types in Kotlin can be nullable, and only then can they have a null value assigned. Nullable types are declared with a question mark at the end. First, take a look at this example where the compiler doesn't allow a non-nullable type to be assigned a null value:

```
var error: String = null //Compiler error
```

If you declare your type as nullable, with a question mark, then the compiler allows assigning nulls:

```
var nullable: String? = null
```

If you try to access a variable of a nullable type in your source code, the compiler will not allow it, because during compile time we don't know if this value will be safe to access, that is, not null.

That's why Kotlin has several operators for dealing with nullable types. The first one is safe call operator ? . It combines a null check and a member access into a single declaration.

First, take a look how would you check, without this operator, if it is safe to access a nullable type:

```
fun nullCheck(str: String?) {
    val upperCase: String? = if (str != null) {
        str.toUpperCase()
    }
     else {
        null
    }
}
```

Thanks to safe call operator, this can be done with one line of code:

```
fun safeCall(str: String?) {
    val upperCase: String? = str?.toUpperCase()
}
```

You can also chain safe call operators, as long they return nullable values:

```
fun safeCallChaining(str: String?) {
    val firstLetterCapitalized: String? = str?.take(1)?.toUpperCase()
}
```

There is also an operator for making non-null assertions. It is expressed with two exclamation marks, `!!`, and it converts a nullable type into non-nullable. If you use it on a null value then a null pointer exception is thrown. Take a look at this example: if you pass a string object to this function, it will be printed out in upper case. But when a null value is passed, the runtime throws a `KotlinNullPointerException` on the first line of the function, when you use the non-null assertion:

```
fun nonNullAssertion(str: String?) {
    val nonNullString = str!!
    val upperCase: String = nonNullString.toUpperCase()
    println(upperCase)
}
```

With this operator, you are in full control of nullability and you are basically telling the compiler *I know this value will not be null, give me access to it.*

In general, you should you use the safe call operator if you can.

Kotlin also has the so-called **Elvis** operator `?:` which is similar to Java's ternary operator.

It can only be used on nullable expressions and it is used to provide a default value in case the expression is null. In this example, we want to assign to a local variable string in upper case if it is not null, and if it is null, just an empty string. Instead of using an `if-else` expression, with the Elvis operator it looks like this:

```
fun elvisOperator(str: String?) {
    val upperCase = str?.toUpperCase() ?: ""
}
```

Basically what the Elvis operator does is evaluate the left side of the operator. If it is not null, this value is used, if it is null the right side of the operator is evaluated. You can put literals, properties or function calls on the right side . You can also chain them, as this example shows:

```
fun chainingElvisOperator(first: String?, second:String?) {
    val upperCase = first?.toUpperCase() ?: second?.toUpperCase() ?: ""
}
```

Casting

To cast from one type to another, Kotlin uses the `as` keyword. Here's how you would cast `Any` type to an `Int` type:

```
fun casting(any: Any) {
    val num = any as Int
}
```

During runtime, before casting, the JVM will check if the source type can be cast to target type. If not, `ClassCastException` will be thrown.

Safe casting

There is also the safe casting operator, `as?`. This operator checks, before casting, whether or not types are compatible. If they are, then it works as a normal `as` operator. If not, a null value is assigned. Notice how in this example, the local variable num has to be declared as a nullable type:

```
fun safeCasting(any: Any) {
    val num: Int? = any as? Int
}
```

Safe casts can be used with all other null handling operators (safe call, non-null assertions, and Elvis), but Elvis is probably the most useful one. Together they can be used to do a non-null try-cast operation, like this example shows:

```
fun safeCastingWithElvisl(any: Any) {
    val num: Int = any as? Int ?: 0
}
```

Control flow

Kotlin has statements for determining what sections of the code will be executed next, during the runtime of a program. These statements are known as control flow statements.

These statments are:

1. If-else
2. When
3. Loops
4. for loops
5. while loops
6. do-while loops

if-else

Kotlin's `if-else` statements are expressions, not keywords. Which means they can have a value. Consider this example where an if-else expression is used to initialize a variable:

```
val str: String = if (num < 10) "Lower than 10" else "Equal or greater than 10"
```

When

Kotlin doesn't have switch statements, like Java and other popular languages. Switch in other languages is a conditional operator which can be used for comparing multiple conditions on a variable.

In Kotlin this operator is called `when` and does the same job as a switch in other languages.

It checks the variable value against multiple conditions, and, if a condition is satisfied, it executes the expression for that branch. `when` is a lot more powerful than Java's switch operator. `when` in Kotlin is an expression, which means it can also return values.

If `when` is used as a statement, then it doesn't have to be exhaustive, that is, not all branches have to be covered, as this example shows:

```
fun checkNumbers(num: Int) {
    when(num) {
        1 -> println("Number is 1")
        2,3,4,5 -> println("Number is in range from 2 to 5")
    }
}
```

If you are using `when` as an expression, then it has to be exhaustive, that is, the compiler has to be sure that all possible branches are covered, as you can see in this example:

```
fun checkNumbersExhaustive(num: Int): String {
    return when(num) {
        1 -> "Number is 1"
        2,3,4,5 -> "Number is in range from 2 to 5"
        else -> "Number is higher than 5"
    }
}
```

`when` accepts any object as its argument, unlike Java's `switch`, which accepts only `enums`, strings and numbers. Here you can see how `when` can be used for type checking:

```
fun whenAny(any: Any) {
    when (any) {
        is Int -> println("This is an Int type")
        is Double -> println("This is a Double type")
        is String -> println("This is a String type")
    }
}
```

You can also use when without arguments. You can test against arbitrary boolean conditions inside it. Consider the following example:

```
fun whenWithoutArgument(a: Int, b: Int) {
    when {
        a * b > 100 -> println("product of a and b is more than 100")
        a + b > 100 -> println("sum of a and b is more than 100")
        a < b -> println("a is less than b")
    }
}
```

Loops

Kotlin supports standard loops that also exist in other languages, like Java, C++, and others. This includes for loops, while loops and do-while loops.

For loops

For loops have a slightly different syntax than in other languages (Java, C#, C++). Index based for loops, like those found in other languages don't exist in Kotlin. In Kotlin you use for loop for iterating over anything that provides an Iterable interface. The next example shows how to loop from 0 to 10 and print these numbers out (10 is included):

```
for (i: Int in 0..10) {
    println(i)
}
```

The .. syntax creates an IntRange type which implements the Iterable interface, in other words, it can be iterated over. For loops always use the in keyword for iteration. This keyword can also be used to check if a value is contained inside an Iterable interface:

```
if (5 in 1..10) print("5 found in range")
```

Type inference also works inside for loop syntax, and specifying (an Int type in this case) is optional:

```
for (i in 0..10) {
    println(i)
}
```

The same syntax applies for looping over any other Iterable interface (Arrays, Collections from Java standard library and others). Here's how you would loop over an array of integers:

```
val array = arrayOf(1, 2, 3)
for (i in array) println (i)
```

If you don't want to include the last number in the range, you can then build it with an until extension function from the Kotlin Standard Library. The following example prints out numbers from 1 to 4:

```
for (i in 1 until 5) {
    println(i)
}
```

If you need to iterate over a range in reverse order, you can build them with the `downTo` function. This example prints out numbers from 5 to 1 (1 is included):

```
fun downToLoop() {
    for (i in 5 downTo 1) {
        println(i)
    }
}
```

While loops

While loops are the same as in other languages, they will loop until the boolean condition in `while` is met:

```
var i = 0
while (i < 10) {
    println("value is $i")
    i += 1
}
```

Do-While loops

The do-while loop is similar to `while`, the difference is that the do-while loop will always enter the statement, unlike the while loop which might never execute the loop if the `while` statement is false on start.

```
do {
    println("This will be printed only once")
} while (false)
```

Exceptions

With exception handling features of a language, you can deal with unpredicted situations or exceptional states that can occur while your code is executing. Kotlin is no different from other languages, like C# and Java and has the same keywords for handling exceptions. These are `try`, `catch`, and `finally`. With these keywords, you can execute a function or some other action which may fail, execute some code in case of failure, and do a cleanup of resources.

```
val file = File("foo")
var stream: OutputStream? = null
try {
```

```
        stream = file.outputStream()
        //do something with stream
    } catch (ex: FileNotFoundException) {
        println("File doesn't exist")
    } finally {
        if (stream != null) stream.close()
    }
```

When you detect an error, or an exceptional state has occurred, you can tell that to the runtime by raising an exception. The caller of your function can catch that exception and try to recover it from an exceptional state. If he doesn't, then the exception is thrown further up the function call stack.

Exceptions are raised with the `throw` keyword. You can create your own Exception types by extending the base Exception class from the Java standard library or by implementing the throwable interface. You'll learn more about extending classes and implementing interfaces in the next chapter. Most of the time, creating your own Exception type will not be needed. The Java and Kotlin Standard Libraries have numerous Exception types that cover most common programming errors. This is how you would throw an exception if a number is not in the range from 1 to 10:

```
if (num !in 1..10) throw IllegalArgumentException("Number has to be from 1
to 10")
```

Both `try` and `throws` keywords in Kotlin are expressions, that is, they can return a value. The following example shows how `throws` can be used as an expression:

```
val divide = if (divisor > 0) {
    value / divisor
} else {
    throw IllegalArgumentException("Can't divide with 0")
}
```

Finally, Kotlin doesn't have checked exceptions. Checked exceptions are a type of exception that have to be either declared or caught in the function in which they are thrown. In other words, they have to be handled explicitly.

Not many other languages have checked exceptions, but Java is one of them. If you don't want to ignore the exception, then Java requires a lot of code just to rethrow the exception in a catch block.

Since Kotlin doesn't have checked exceptions, you don't have to catch them. For example, if you are calling a Java function that throws a checked exception, the Kotlin compiler will not force you to wrap the function call inside a `try`/`catch` block, like the Java compiler would.

Equality comparison

If you are familiar with Java, then you know that the == operator on reference types is used for comparing reference (memory address) equality. If you want to compare structural equality, you should call the equals method from the base Object class.

Kotlin overrides the == operator so that it calls the equals method, that is, it is used for structural comparison. If you want to compare two objects for reference equality in Kotlin, then you can use the three equals signs, the === operator and !== for a negation of reference equality:

```
val a = "Kotlin"
val b = "Kotlin"
val c = "Java"
println("Strings a and b are equal in content: ${a == b}")
println("Strings b and c are equal in reference: ${b === c}")
```

Packages

Java uses packages to organize classes. Kotlin also has packages and they work in the same way. The biggest difference from Java is that declaring a package is optional. In Kotlin you can have a file or a class without a package.

Package declaration has to be at the top of the file. If you want to use other types that are declared in the same package, then you can access them directly. If they are declared in another package, then you have to import them first. The following example shows a package and import declarations. It shows how a package is declared on the top, uses an import from the Java standard library and declares a function on a file level:

```
package quickstartguide.kotlin.chapter2

import java.lang.Math.PI

fun circumference(radius: Double): Double {
    return 2 * PI * radius
}
```

Unlike Java, where you import classes, Kotlin allows importing of any kind of declarations.

If you were to import the circumference function from the preceding example, it would look like this:

```
import quickstartguide.kotlin.chapter2.circumference

val circ = circumference(10.0)
```

You can also import every declaration from a package with the wildcard imports. If you were to declare this inside a file, this is what you would use:

```
import java.util.*
```

You'd have access to every declaration inside the java.util package.

Visibility modifiers

Visibility modifiers define how your declarations are accessible from other classes and packages. In Kotlin you can use the same modifiers that are found in Java, private, protected, and public.

Private visibility modifiers restrict access to the same class or a file. And public opens the access to everybody, no matter where they are trying to access a member from.

Java also has a fourth visibility modifier, package-private, which is also a default visibility modifier (if you don't specify a visibility modifier, then package-private is implicitly applied). Package-private in Java means that declarations are visible only inside the same package. It is easy to bypass this visibility modifier. In your code, you can declare a package with the same name as the one you wish to import from and thus break the access restriction. This is one of the reasons Kotlin doesn't have the package-private modifier. Instead, Kotlin has a similar one, internal. Internal restricts visibility to the same modules. Definition of a module varies per build system, but it can be described as a single compilation unit. In Gradle, this would be a Gradle module or a project.

Since internal is not available in Java, it also doesn't exist in Java bytecode. So the Kotlin compiler is responsible for enforcing its access rules. Internal is compiled to public in Java bytecode, which means that anybody will be allowed to call your internal Kotlin code from Java.

Kotlin, being an object-oriented language, allows you to use visibility modifiers on fields, properties, functions, interfaces, and classes. The default visibility modifier in Kotlin is public.

Another difference from Java is that, in Kotlin, the private modifier declared on a file level is visible to all declarations in that file. As this example shows:

```
private fun sayMyName(name: String) {
    println(name)
}

fun accessPrivateFunc() {
    sayMyName("John")
}
```

The following table summarizes all Kotlin visibility modifiers:

Modifier	Visibility
private	inside the same class or a file
protected	inside subclasses
internal	inside same module
public (default)	everywhere

Summary

In this chapter, you learned about the fundamental building blocks of the Kotlin language. We covered the basics, like variables, functions, and control flow statements. We also learned about the basic types Kotlin uses and we've seen how Kotlin tries to improve Java's shortcomings with its null safety features.

Now you should be able to start using the language on your own and, if you have experience with other languages (especially Java), you could already see what sets Kotlin apart from them.

In the next chapter, you will learn about classes and object-oriented programming with Kotlin.

Classes and Object-Oriented Programming

Kotlin is an **object-oriented** (**OO**) language, and classes are the main element of an OO language. This chapter will delve into the details of working with classes in Kotlin.

Even if you have experience with Java or similar languages, you can still learn from this chapter. There are a lot of differences from Java when working with classes, such as the constructor syntax, default visibility modifiers, properties, and so on. Kotlin also has some unique features not found in other languages, such as sealed and data classes.

In this chapter, you will learn about the following:

- Classes
- Properties
- Class constructors
- Nested classes
- Enum classes
- Data classes
- Inheritance
- Overriding members
- Abstract classes
- Interfaces
- Interfaces versus abstract classes
- The object keyword
- Class delegation
- Sealed classes
- Smart casts

Classes

To begin with classes, let's take a look how Java would declare a class, with a couple of fields that are initialized in the class constructor. To enforce encapsulation, the class has private fields but provides get and set methods for each field, so they can be accessed and modified from outside:

```
public final class User {
    private String firstName;
    private String lastName;
    private int birthYear;

public User(String firstName, String lastName, int birthYear) {
        this.firstName = firstName;
        this.lastName = lastName;
        this.birthYear = birthYear;
        }

    public String getFirstName() {
        return firstName;
        }

    public void setFirstName(String firstName) {
        this.firstName = firstName;
        }

    public String getLastName() {
        return lastName;
        }

    public void setLastName(String lastName) {
        this.lastName = lastName;
        }

    public int getBirthYear() {
        return birthYear;
        }

    public void setBirthYear(int birthYear) {
        this.birthYear = birthYear;
        }
}
```

Now, the same class written in Kotlin would look like this:

```
class User(var firstName: String,
           var lastName: String,
           var birthYear: String)
```

It may be hard to believe that the classes are considered equal; after all, the Java class has almost 30 lines of code and the Kotlin class would be only one line if we didn't use line breaks. But, if we take a look at the Java bytecode that the Kotlin compiler will produce for this class, we'll see that in fact they are equal. There is only one difference: the Kotlin class will have a couple of lines of Java bytecode more because we used non-nullable types in Kotlin, and the Kotlin compiler emits assertions that check arguments passed to functions are not null.

Now that we have seen how Kotlin is more concise than Java, let's explore the details.

Properties

A Kotlin class doesn't have `setter` or `getter` methods, yet it doesn't break encapsulation by exposing private fields. The reason is that Kotlin has properties. C# is one of the languages Kotlin drew inspiration from, and the concept of properties is one of the things it took from C#. You can think of properties as fields and methods, all in one place. To the outside users of a property, the syntax looks like they are accessing a public field of a class. Internally in your class, behind a property, you can have get and set accessors or methods and a private backing field. The `get` and `set` methods then control how your private field is accessed, thus not breaking encapsulation.

Specifying get and set, as in our case, is optional. If you omit them, then it is implied that the property is both read and write. The compiler generates a private backing field for you in that case. You can also have get only accessor inside a property. This is then considered a read-only property and it cannot be modified from outside. You can also have a set-only property, which is considered write-only and cannot be read from outside. Finally, you can declare your properties with the `val` keyword, and with this you make them immutable from both inside the containing class and outside the class.

The following examples summarize the get and set accessors.

Get only property, without compiler generated field. We use our own backing _name property here:

```
private var _name: String = ""

var name: String = _name
    get() {
            println("name property is being accessed")
             return _name
    }
```

Set only property, again without an implicit backing field. The set accessor accepts a parameter that is the same type as the containing property. You can name this parameter (type inference also works on properties and their accessors, so you can omit the type) whatever you like, but the convention is to name it value:

```
private var _name: String = ""

var name: String = _name
    set(value) {
        println("name property is being set with value: $value")
        _name = value
    }
```

And both get and set accessors. This example uses the implicit compiler generated field, which can be accessed with the field keyword:

```
var name: String = ""
    get() {
        println("name property is being accessed")
        return field
    }
    set(value) {
        println("name property is being set with value: $value")
        field = value
    }
```

Properties always have to be initialized, the same as local variables, unless you use a get and set property without the implicit backing field, as this example shows:

```
private var _name: String = ""

var name: String //doesn't have to be initialized
    get() {
        println("name property is being accessed")
        return _name
    }
```

```
set(value) {
    println("name property is being set with value: $value")
    _name = value
}
```

Set and get methods can have visibility modifiers. If you don't specify a visibility modifier, then a default, public modifier is implicitly applied. So, it is perfectly fine to have a public property with a private set method. This implies that the property's get method is visible from outside, and the set method is only visible inside the class, that is, only the class itself can modify it:

```
var name: String = ""
    private set
```

In this example, you can also see that specifying parentheses, a parameter name, and curly braces are optional.

Finally, we have to mention the `lateinit` keyword. We already said how properties and fields have to be initialized when they are declared. Sometimes when declaring properties, their values will be known only after a class has been initialized. Dependency injection is one of these cases, where usually an inversion of control container sets the values or injects them after the constructor of a class has been called. In that case, you would declare your field as nullable and initialize it with null. But, then you would have to use null safety operators, even though you know that the field is never null. To save you from these kinds of situations, Kotlin offers the `lateinit` keyword. It can only be applied to properties and fields. The keyword allows you to have a member declared, but not initialized:

```
private lateinit var name: String
```

`Lateinit` is allowed only on reference types and non-null properties. You'll get a compiler error if you put `lateinit` on a primitive or nullable property:

```
private lateinit var birthYear: Int // compiler error
private lateinit var lastName: String? // compiler error
```

If you try to use a `lateinit` property that has not been initialized, Kotlin will throw a runtime exception. You can check whether a member has been initialized with the `isInitialized` extension function. The function has to specify a receiver and property. In the following example, the `this` keyword means the receiver is the class we are calling the function, and after two colons comes the property:

```
fun checkIfLateinitSet() {
    val initialized = this::name.isInitialized
}
```

Class constructors

In Kotlin, class constructors can be defined in two ways, as primary and as secondary constructors.

Primary constructors

Kotlin has two ways of declaring a constructor. In the example of the User class, we had a primary constructor. Primary constructors are declared with parentheses after the class name, in the class header.

Specifying the constructor keyword is optional if the constructor doesn't have visibility modifiers or annotations.

Constructors can have parameters, but cannot have any initialization code in them. The Java User class constructor has both parameters and initialization code. Initialization code was needed because the private fields needed to be initialized with values from constructor arguments.

The same code was not needed in Kotlin, because Kotlin allows properties to be declared inside the constructor. When declared like this, they become both properties and constructor parameters. The Kotlin compiler then emits bytecode that resembles the Java user class. It will have fields and a constructor with parameters that initialize the fields. Properties declared inside a constructor can also have visibility modifiers applied to them. We don't have any; they are implicitly public. Here's how you would declare a class with a private constructor-declared property:

```
class PrivateProperty(private val num: Int)
```

If you want, you can have only constructor parameters without them being properties. In that case, you have to omit the var or val keyword from the parameter names.

If you need to do some initialization logic, a class body can have an init block in which you can access constructor parameters and do additional object initialization. Let's now write the User class again, with the initializer, and with properties this time declared inside the class body:

```
class User(firstName: String,
           lastName: String,
           birthYear: Int) {
    var firstName: String
    var lastName: String
    var birthYear: Int
```

```
    init {
        println("Calling constructor of User class")
        this.firstName = firstName
        this.lastName = lastName
        this.birthYear = birthYear
    }
}
```

This is code is equal to the initial `User` class we wrote in Kotlin, with one addition that this class prints out to the output each time it is constructed. The init block would otherwise be redundant because we can also initialize the members of a class inline, that is, we can access constructor arguments when initializing the members, as the following example shows:

```
class User(firstName: String,
           lastName: String,
           birthYear: Int) {
    var firstName: String = firstName
    var lastName: String = lastName
    var birthYear: Int = birthYear
}
```

You can have as may init blocks as you want, and they will all be called in the order they were declared, as this example shows:

```
class MultipleInits {
    private var counter = 1

    init {
        //called first
        println("I'm called $counter time(s)")
    }

    init {
        //called second
        println("I'm called $counter time(s)")
    }
}
```

Secondary constructors

There are also secondary constructors; the syntax is similar to primary constructors. The difference is that secondary constructors are declared inside the class body:

```
class User {

    constructor(firstName: String,
```

```
                    lastName: String,
                    birthYear: Int) {
    }
}
```

Secondary constructors cannot have properties, only constructor parameters. If you need to initialize your fields with constructor parameters, you can do that inside the `init` block.

You can also have both primary and secondary constructors inside the same class. In that case, the secondary constructor has to call the primary one. This is done with the colon and the `this` keyword after the secondary constructor declaration:

```
class User(firstName: String,
           lastName: String) {

    constructor(firstName: String,
                lastName: String,
                birthYear: Int) : this(firstName, lastName) {
    }
}
```

Kotlin allows only one primary constructor, but you can have as many secondary constructors as you want:

```
class User {
    constructor(firstName: String,
                lastName: String) {

    }

    constructor(firstName: String,
                lastName: String,
                birthYear: Int) {
    }
}
```

Notice how it is not needed to call other secondary constructors. Only the primary constructor has to be called from the secondary ones.

Final by default

Java classes can be declared with final keyword, which prohibits other classes from inheriting from that class. Kotlin doesn't have this modifier, because all classes are implicitly final in Kotlin.

If you want to make your class extendable, that is, make it possible for other classes to inherit from your class, you have to explicitly mark it with the `open` keyword.

Constructing class instances

Kotlin doesn't have the `new` keyword, like Java or C# have. If you want to construct a class in Kotlin, you call its constructor like you would call a function. Here's how we would create an instance of our `User` class:

```
val user = User("Bruce", "Wayne", "1950")
```

Nested classes

Kotlin allows classes to be declared inside the body of another class. Other modern OO languages also allow this, and these kinds of classes are usually called nested or inner classes. Here's an example of how you would declare a nested class:

```
class User(val name: String) {
    class Address(val street: String,
                  val streetNumber: String,
                  val zip: String,
                  val city: String)
}
```

And if you'd like to instantiate the Address class, you would have to do it like this, prefixing the containing class first:

```
val address = User.Address("Aparo Park", "1", "ABC", "Gotham City")
```

Visibility modifiers can be applied to nested classes as well. Here's the same example, but this time the nested class is private:

```
class User(val name: String) {
    private class Address(val street: String,
                          val streetNumber: String,
                          val zip: String,
                          val city: String)


    private val address = Address("Aparo Park", "1", "ABC", "Gotham City")
}
```

Now the `Address` class cannot be instantiated like in the previous example, because it is visible only inside the `User` class. Also, the property address has to be private, otherwise it would expose the private class to the outside and the compiler will not allow this.

Java also supports nested classes, and in Java they can access the containing class and its members by default (nested classes have an implicit reference to the outer containing class). Java also allows nested classes to have a static modifier. In that case, they don't have an implicit reference to the outer containing class.

Kotlin's nested classes have the opposite as the default. They don't hold an implicit reference to the outer class. If you want to enable this, you have to add the inner keyword to your nested class. The following example illustrates this:

```kotlin
class User(val name: String) {
    class Address(val street: String,
            val streetNumber: String,
            val zip: String,
            val city: String) {
        init {
            // compiler error, can't access name property
            println("The name of the User is: $name")
        }
    }
}
```

If you add the inner keyword, you can access members from the outer class:

```kotlin
class User(val name: String) {

    inner class Address(val street: String,
                val streetNumber: String,
                val zip: String,
                val city: String) {

        init {
            //we can access the name property from the outer class
            println("The name of the User is: $name")
        }
    }
}
```

Enum classes

Enumeration types are used to define a set of named constants. Kotlin, same as Java has an enumeration type, the enum class. Let's say that you want to define a type that represents all months in a year. Yes, you could create a normal class with one property, month name, which is of String type. But, then you would have to guard against invalid month name assignments and throw exceptions in such cases. The class would be error-prone and users of your class wouldn't be happy. This is a perfect use case for the enum class, and here is how you would define an enum type to represent all the months of the year:

```
enum class Month {
    JANUARY,
    FEBRUARY,
    MARCH,
    APRIL,
    MAY,
    JUNE,
    JULY,
    AUGUST,
    SEPTEMBER,
    OCTOBER,
    NOVEMBER,
    DECEMBER
}
```

Now you can't have invalid months, and if you want to assign a month type to a variable, you can only choose from the constants we have defined:

```
val march = Month.MARCH
```

Enum classes, both in Kotlin and in Java, are full-blown classes, so they can have members, that is, properties and functions. This makes them more powerful than enumeration types in some other languages, C# for example. C#'s enums are value types; by default, the underlying type of each constant is a 32-bit integer and they cannot have members.

We could make our Month enum class more usable; we could also add a numerical representation of each month to the type. Since enum types are classes, they can also have constructors. In fact, Kotlin will allow us to have both primary and secondary constructors and init blocks inside an enum. Here's how you would add a property of Int type to our enum class that represents Month numerically:

```
enum class Month2 (val num: Int) {
    JANUARY(1),
    FEBRUARY(2),
    MARCH(3),
    APRIL(4),
    MAY(5),
    JUNE(6),
    JULY(7),
    AUGUST(8),
    SEPTEMBER(9),
    OCTOBER(10),
    NOVEMBER(11),
    DECEMBER(12)
}
```

This integer constructor property is only needed when defining a constant inside this enum. You would then assign a Month enum constant like in the previous example. And, when you have an actual constant, from it you can access all the members that enum type defines. Here's how you would access the numerical representation of our Month enum:

```
val may = Month2.MAY
val mayNum = may.num
```

The enum class type also has two helper methods. The first one is for getting an array of all defined constants. We use it here to print out all the months:

```
for (month in Month.values()) {
    println(month)
}
```

The second one is for getting an enum object from the constant string value. This is how we would get the month of June, by passing a string to the valueOf function:

```
val june = Month.valueOf("JUNE")
```

Data classes

Data classes are one more concept that Kotlin uses to be a more productive language. To show this, let's go back to our User class in Java. If we wanted to compare this type by the values it holds (its properties), we would have to override the equals method and compare all the values inside it. But then, with the equals method overridden, we also have to override the hashcode method; otherwise, none of the hash-related collection types (HashMap, HashSet, HashTable, and so on) would work. The hashcode method should return an equal hash value from all objects that the equals method considers the same. While we are overriding those two methods, let's also override the toString method so that the users of our class can get a nice string representation of it. Then, the Java version would look like this (getter and setter methods omitted):

```java
public final class User {
    private String firstName;
    private String lastName;
    private int birthYear;

    public User(String firstName, String lastName, int birthYear) {
        this.firstName = firstName;
        this.lastName = lastName;
        this.birthYear = birthYear;
    }

    @Override
    public boolean equals(Object obj) {
        if (obj instanceof User) {
            User other = (User)obj;
            return this.firstName.equals(other.firstName)
                    && this.lastName.equals(other.lastName)
                    && this.birthYear == other.birthYear;
        }
        return false;
    }

    @Override
    public int hashCode() {
        int result = 31;
        result = 31 * result + this.firstName.hashCode();
        result = 31 * result + this.lastName.hashCode();
        result = 31 * result + birthYear;
        return result;
    }

    @Override
    public String toString() {
```

```
            return "User(firstName="+this.firstName
                    + ", lastName=" + this.lastName
                    + ", birthYear=" + this.birthYear
                    + ")";
    }
}
```

But in Kotlin, thanks to data classes, the equivalent code would look like this:

```
data class User(var firstName: String,
                var lastName: String,
                var birthYear: String)
```

Again, if we didn't break the lines for readability, the Kotlin code could be only one line. And yes, only adding the `data` keyword in front of the class will tell the Kotlin compiler to produce in the bytecode all the code we had to type in the Java version.

When you declare a data class, the compiler implements the `hashcode`, `equals`, and `toString` functions for you. It also adds one more that we don't have in our Java version. That is the `copy` function. Sometimes, there is a need to get a copy of an object and at the same time modify some of its properties. If we wanted to copy our user and change only his first name, we'd do it like this:

```
val user = User("Bruce", "Wayne", "1965")
val userCopy = user.copy("John")
```

This code will produce a compiler warning. The copy function should use named arguments (we'll learn about them in the next chapter). The proper way would be to specify the name of the argument we are changing, like this:

```
val user = User("Bruce", "Wayne", "1965")
val userCopy = user.copy(firstName = "John")
```

By default, the Kotlin compiler will generate all the functions we have mentioned. But if you want to have your own version of any of these functions, you just have to implement it yourself in your data class. When the compiler sees that you overrode such a method, it'll skip adding it and the one you've provided will be used.

Finally, we have to mention the restrictions on using data classes:

- It cannot be an open, sealed, or abstract class
- The primary constructor parameters have to be properties, that is, they have to have the `val` or `var` keyword
- The primary constructor has to have at least one property

Inheritance

Inheritance is one of the main aspects of object-oriented programming. Basically, it allows classes (subclasses) to inherit members from base types (superclasses). They usually have their own functions and properties, which are not found in the base type. With inheritance, you can achieve code reuse, build class hierarchies, or extend base types with additional functionality.

Let's take a look at an example. We have the old User class we used in this chapter, and let's say we also need to have a class that represents administrator users, which will have the same properties as the base User class plus one additional property, role. We can say this would be a good use of inheritance, so let's create the AdminUser class, which extends the base User class:

```
open class User(var firstName: String,
                var lastName: String,
                var birthYear: String)

class AdminUser(firstName: String,
                lastName: String,
                birthYear: String,
                var role: String): User(firstName, lastName, birthYear)
```

You can see that we marked the base `User` class with the `open` keyword. This is needed because classes in Kotlin are `final` (not inheritable) by default.

The actual inheritance syntax is expressed with a colon after the class declaration. After the colon comes the type we wish to inherit from.

Another thing you can see in the syntax is that we called the base type constructor and passed the three required parameters. When inheriting from a class that has a primary constructor, you always have to call it in that place.

If a base class has only secondary constructors, then you can call them from the inheriting class with the `super` keyword:

```
open class User {

    constructor(firstName: String,
                lastName: String,
                birthYear: String)
}

class AdminUser : User {
    constructor(firstName: String,
```

```
        lastName: String,
        birthYear: String,
        role: String) : super(firstName, lastName, birthYear)
}
```

The constructor parameters needed for the base type are also present in the inherited class, but note that they are not properties there (they don't have the var or val keywords).

Kotlin wouldn't allow this, since it would mean that we are then overriding the base type's properties. Kotlin, the same as Java, doesn't support multiple inheritance, that is, you can inherit only from one class.

Overriding members

Reimplementing functions or properties from a base type is called overriding. Overriding is also a way to achieve polymorphism, another aspect of object-oriented programming. In Kotlin, you can override them only if the base type allows it. By default, all members in Kotlin are final, that is, cannot be overridden. To allow a subclass to override a member, it has to have the open keyword. This is in contrast to Java, where by default every member is overridable. Another difference from Java is that whenever you are overriding a member, you have to have the override keyword present. Java doesn't have such a keyword and overriding is considered with just declaring a function with the same name and signatures as the base type. This can be error-prone and that's why Java uses the @Override annotation to make the developer's intentions clearer:

```
open class Base {
    open fun print() {
        println("I'm called from the base type")
    }
}

class Derived : Base() {
    override fun print() {
        println("I'm called from the super type")
    }
}
```

Members that have the override keyword are implicitly open, that is, they can be overridden by their subclasses. If you want to prevent further overriding, you can apply a `final` keyword to it:

```
open class Derived : Base() {
    final override fun print() {

        println("I'm called from the super type")
    }
}
```

You can also override properties, and the syntax is the same as for functions. But, note that you can have `open` and `override` keywords present in the primary constructor:

```
open class User(open val name: String)

class AdminUser(override var name: String) : User(name)
```

Notice that you can override an immutable property with a mutable one. This is allowed because `val` means that there is a getter function only on the property, and `var` would add a setter function in the derived class. But, overriding `var` with `val` is not allowed.

Abstract classes

The `abstract` keyword in Kotlin defines a class or a member whose implementation is missing or incomplete. Abstract classes can be extended but cannot be instantiated. Abstract classes do not have to have abstract members, but an abstract member has to be defined inside an abstract class. Let's define an abstract class that has two abstract members, a property and a function:

```
abstract class BaseUser {
    abstract val name: String
    abstract fun login()

    fun logout(){
        println("Logging out")
    }
}
```

You can see that we also have one non-abstract function. Abstract classes can have state and non-abstract members. You can also see that an abstract function doesn't have an implementation, it only has a signature. The same for the abstract property, it doesn't return any value. If you had the abstract modifier on a member that has an implementation, you'd get a compiler error. This `BaseUser` class wouldn't compile:

```
abstract class BaseUser {

    //compiler error
    abstract val name: String = ""

    //compiler error
    abstract fun login() {
            //login the user
    }

    fun logout(){
        println("Logging out")
    }
}
```

Now, let's create a class that inherits from our abstract class. All the members that are marked with the abstract keyword have to be implemented, that is, overridden by the class that extends the abstract class:

```
class User(override val name: String) : BaseUser() {

    override fun login(){
        println("Logging out")
    }
}
```

Interfaces

If you have any experience with any modern language, then you have probably used a type that defines a behavior. These types are called traits in Scala, protocols in Swift, and interfaces in Kotlin, Java, and C#.

An interface is a blueprint or a definition of a type. When a type implements an interface, we can then refer to it by this contract, that is, a set of methods that the type implements.

Here is an interface declaration in Kotlin:

```
interface Drivable {
    fun drive()
}
```

The syntax for implementing an interface is the same as for inheritance. In the implementing class header, after a primary constructor or a class name comes the colon and the interface name:

```
class Car : Drivable {
    override fun drive() {
        println("Driving a car")
    }
}
```

The only difference from inheritance syntax is that we don't call the base type constructor because interfaces don't have one.

The implementing type (unless it is an abstract class) has to implement or override all the members that interface defined. Otherwise, you'd get a compiler error.

Interfaces in Kotlin, the same as in Java (since Java 8), can have default method implementations. Consider this interface:

```
interface Flyable {
    fun climb() {
        println("Climbing")
    }

    fun fly()
}
```

Now, all the implementing classes only have to override the function, without the default implementation:

```
class AirPlane : Flyable {
    override fun fly() {
        println("Flying a plane")
    }
}
```

But if you wish, you can also override the function that has a default implementation:

```
class Drone : Flyable {
    override fun climb() {
        println("Climbing slowly")
    }

    override fun fly() {
        println("Flying a plane")
    }
}
```

You can also define a property inside an interface in Kotlin, as this example shows:

```
interface Ridable {
    fun ride()
    val name: String
}
```

Finally, we have to mention that visibility modifiers that can be applied to classes can also be applied to an interface. But, interface members cannot have private or protected visibility modifiers. They can only have public (which is default) and internal.

Interfaces versus abstract classes

Now that we've covered both abstract classes and interfaces, you might be wondering what you should use when you are building your app. They look similar in some ways, but there are some important differences that we'll cover now, which will make it easier for you to choose which one to use.

We've already mentioned that Kotlin doesn't allow multiple inheritance. Take a look at this example:

```
abstract class InsureBase {
    abstract fun insure()
}

abstract class CarBase {
    abstract fun drive()
}

//compiler error, can't inherit from multiple classes
class InsurableCar: InsureBase(), CarBase() {
    override fun insure() {
    }
```

```
    override fun drive() {
    }
}
```

This won't compile, because we are trying to inherit from two classes.

Interfaces don't have that limitation; a class can implement as many interfaces as it wants. So, if we want to have a type that can be both driven and insured, we can have two interfaces that define that behavior and one concrete class that implements them both:

```
interface Insurable {
    fun insure()
}

interface Drivable {
    fun drive()
}

class InsurableSuperCar: Insurable, Drivable {
    override fun insure() {
        println("Car is now insured")
    }

    override fun drive() {
        println("Car is driving")
    }
}
```

Another difference between the two is that abstract classes can have state. Abstract classes can have fields and properties, and functions that modify them. Interfaces, on the other hand, can have only function or property signatures. If you want to achieve code reuse, then this makes abstract classes a better choice.

Finally, when talking about relationships between types and whether interfaces or abstract classes should be used, usually the relationship can be broken down to **is-a** and **can-do** relationships. We can explain this better if we use types from the Java standard library. For example, the library has an abstract class called AbstractList. The class provides an implementation that is used in classes that extend it, such as ArrayList and LinkedList. When talking about ArrayList, we can always say that ArrayList is also an AbstractList.

The library also has an Iterable interface. This one has the only method, iterator(), which should return an iterator object. This interface says a type can be iterated over, so we can say this is a can-do functionality.

Object keyword

Kotlin has an `object` keyword, which combines both declaring a class and creating an instance of it in one action. It can be used in three different situations and has three different meanings. Let's take a look at all of them:

- **Object declaration**: Defines a singleton class.
- **Companion object**: Defines a nested class that can hold members related to the outer containing class. These members can't require an instance of the outer class.
- **Object expression**: Creates an instance of the object on the fly, the same as Java's anonymous inner classes.

Singletons with object keyword

Sometimes, your program has to have only one instance of a certain type. This pattern is known as a singleton. In other languages, you would have to implement this pattern manually, making sure that only one instance of your type gets created. But, Kotlin has language support for creating singletons with the object keyword. Here is an example:

```kotlin
object Singleton {
    fun sayMyName() {
       println("I'm a singleton")
    }
}
```

This will both declare a Singleton class and create an instance of it. Notice how we haven't defined a constructor. Since the compiler creates an instance for you, if you tried to declare a constructor or create an instance yourself, you'd get a compiler error:

```kotlin
//compiler error
val singleton = Singleton()
```

If you need to access a member from an object, you can do so by first accessing the object type and then the member you wish to invoke. Here's how to call a function from an object:

```kotlin
Singleton.sayMyName()
```

Other than not having a constructor, there aren't any differences from normal classes. Objects can have properties and functions; they can also implement interfaces and extend other classes. Here is an object that implements the `Runnable` interface:

```
object RunnableSingleton : Runnable {
    override fun run() {
        println("I'm a runnable singleton")
    }
}
```

Kotlin also allows objects to be declared inside classes; then, they become nested singletons.

Nested objects cannot have an inner keyword; they cannot access members from the outer class. Here is how you would declare an object inside a class:

```
class Outer {
    object Singleton {

    }
}
```

Now, let's see what the compiler does when you declare an object. In the case of our Singleton object from the beginning, the compiler would produce Java bytecode similar to this:

```
public final class User {

    public static final User INSTANCE;

    private User() {

    }

    public void sayMyName() {
        System.out.println("I'm a singleton");
    }

    static {
        INSTANCE = new User();
    }
}
```

The compiler creates a public static final field and assigns it an object created inside the static initializer block.

This also tells us how to call an object's members from Java. We need to access the `INSTANCE` public field first, before accessing any members, like this:

```
Singleton.INSTANCE.sayMyName();
```

Finally, if you need to some kind of initialization of your object, you can do it inside the `init` block. The init block will be called when your object gets constructed:

```
object SingletonWithInitializer {
    var name = ""

    init {
        name = "Singleton"
    }
}
```

Companion objects

Java has a static keyword that can be applied to class members. Static members belong to a type, and not to an instance of a type. Kotlin doesn't have a static keyword, but can achieve this kind of functionality with some other language features. A common use case for static functions is grouping some utility functions inside a class. The collections class from the java.util package is a perfect example of this.

You can have this in Kotlin with functions declared at the file level or inside an object.

Another use of static members could be factory methods. This is usually done by hiding the class constructor from the outside with a private access modifier and delegating the instance construction to static methods.

Factory methods can be useful and sometimes they are preferred to having multiple constructors. In Kotlin, companion objects can be used to implement this design pattern.

Here's how a factory method design pattern would be implemented in Kotlin:

```
class User private constructor(val userId: String) {
    companion object {
        fun newUserWithEmail(email: String): User
        {

            return User(email)
```

```
            }

        fun newUserFromUUID(uuid: UUID): User {
            return User(uuid.toString())
        }
    }
}
```

Accessing the companion object and its members is the same as if they were static:

```
val userFromEmail = User.newUserWithEmail("john@mail.com")
val userFromUUID = User.newUserFromUUID(UUID.randomUUID())
```

The same as with normal objects, companion objects cannot have constructors, but can extend other classes and implement interfaces.

Let's see what the compiler does in the case of our User class and its companion object. This is how would it look if it was compiled from Java:

```
public class User {
    private String userId;

    private static final User.Companion COMPANION = new User.Companion();

    private User(String userId) {
        this.userId = userId;
    }

    public static final class Companion {

        private Companion() {

        }

        public static User newUserWithEmail(String email) {
            return new User(email);
        }

        public static User newUserFromUUID(UUID uuid) {
            return new User(uuid.toString());
        }
    }
}
```

From this code, you can also see how you would access a companion object's members from Java: first by accessing the outer type and then the companion public field.

Companion objects can also have names. By default, if you don't specify a name the compiler will name the class companion. Here's a companion object with an explicit name definition:

```
class Outer {
    companion object Inner {
        fun saySomething() {
            println("Hello")
        }
    }
}
```

Changing the name of a companion doesn't change how we access it. We don't have to specify the name of the companion object; it is optional. We can access its members from the outer type, as you can see here:

```
Outer.saySomething()
```

Static with companion objects

Kotlin doesn't have the static keyword, but to achieve compatibility with Java, it provides support for it with annotations. Kotlin provides the `@JvmStatic` and `@JvmField` annotations, which, when applied to a member of a class, make it static.

In this example, the `@JvmStatic` annotation will tell the compiler to compile the annotated function to a static one, and the `@JvmField` will tell the compiler to compile the annotated property to a static field, without getters and setters:

```
class Static {
    companion object {
        // static method
        @JvmStatic
        fun staticFunction() {

        }
        // static field
        @JvmField
        val staticField = 0
    }
}
```

Anonymous objects

The object keyword has one more use, creating anonymous objects. If you are familiar with Java, then you probably had experience with anonymous inner classes. Anonymous objects are similar to them. With them, you create objects on the `fly`. Let's create an anonymous object of a `Runnable` interface:

```
Thread(object : Runnable {
    override fun run() {
        println("I'm created with anonymous object")
    }
}).run()
```

The syntax for creating anonymous objects is similar to singleton objects, but without the name of the object. The name in most cases is not needed. If you need a name for your anonymous object, or need it to store for later use, you can initialize a variable with it. This example shows it:

```
val runnable = object : Runnable {
    override fun run() {
        println("I'm created with anonymous object")
    }
}
```

Anonymous objects are not restricted to interfaces, you can also create classes with them. Here's how you would create an anonymous object of an abstract class. Notice how we had to call the constructor of the class:

```
val writer = object : Writer() {
    override fun write(cbuf: CharArray, off: Int, len: Int) {
        // implementation omitted
    }

    override fun flush() {
        // implementation omitted
    }

    override fun close() {
        // implementation omitted
    }
}
```

Class delegation

Delegation is a design pattern that combines object composition and inheritance. Basically, it is a mechanism where one object delegates actions to another. To see it in action, let's take a look how we would achieve delegation in Java:

```java
public interface Drivable {
    void drive();
}

public class Car implements Drivable {

    @Override
    public void drive() {
        System.out.println("Driving a car");
    }
}

public class Vehicle implements Drivable {
    private Car car;

    public Vehicle(Car car) {
        this.car = car;
    }

    @Override
    public void drive() {
        car.drive();
    }
}

public void driveVehicle() {
    Car car = new Car();
    Vehicle vehicle = new Vehicle(car);
    vehicle.drive(); // with delegation, car.drive() get's called
}
```

In this example, we have the `Drivable` interface and two classes that implement it. The `Vehicle` class doesn't have its own drive functionality; rather, it delegates the drive function to the `Car` object.

If we were to write the same example in Kotlin, it would look like this:

```kotlin
interface Drivable
{

    fun drive()
```

```
}

class Car : Drivable
{
    override fun drive()
        {
        println("Driving a car")
        }
    }

class Vehicle(car: Car) : Drivable by car
```

You can see how the `Vehicle` class doesn't have any of the code that the Java version had. That is because Kotlin has built-in support for delegation. Notice how in the class header of the `Vehicle` class, after the `Drivable` interface, comes the by keyword and the name of the object that we are delegating this interface to. This is all that is needed for the compiler to produce more or less equivalent bytecode to the Java example.

In our example, we used interfaces, but delegation in Kotlin can also be used for classes, that is, you can delegate the inheritance of a class to another object.

Delegation also works with multiple interfaces. This is how you would have a class that delegates two interfaces to other objects:

```
interface Rideable {
    fun ride()
}

interface Chargable {
    fun charge()
}

class Battery : Chargable {
    override fun charge() {
        println("Charging")
    }
}

class Bike : Rideable {
    override fun ride() {
        println("Riding a bike")
    }
}

class ChargableBike(bike: Bike, battery: Battery): Rideable by bike,
Chargable by battery
```

Sealed classes

If you have experience with C#, then the sealed keyword might be confusing to you. C# uses the sealed keyword to prevent inheritance from a class, the same way Java uses final when declaring a class. Sealed classes in Kotlin are used to define restricted class hierarchies.

Sealed classes are similar to enum classes; you use them to define a fixed set of options. But unlike enum classes, where each constant is a single instance, sealed classes can have multiple instances for each option.

This restricted class hierarchy can be really useful when used with when expressions.

Here's an example of a sealed class hierarchy used with a when statement:

```
sealed class SuperHero

class Hulk: SuperHero() {
    fun smashOpponent() {

    }
}
class SuperMan : SuperHero() {
    fun flyToKrypton() {

    }
}
class SpiderMan : SuperHero() {
    fun useSpiderSense() {

    }
}
fun actOnHero(hero: SuperHero) {
    when (hero) {
        is Hulk -> {
            hero.smashOpponent()
        }
        is SuperMan -> {
            hero.flyToKrypton()
        }
        is SpiderMan -> {
            hero.useSpiderSense()
        }
    }
}
```

You define only one sealed class, the one that acts as the base class for your class hierarchy. All other classes that inherit from the sealed classes can be normal classes, data classes, or objects. Inheriting classes have to be declared in the same file as the sealed class.

A sealed class acts as an abstract class and the compiler will not allow you to create an instance of it. Also, it cannot have non-private constructors, because its constructor is private by default.

Smart casts

If you are wondering how, in the previous section, we called functions that belong to supertypes from the base SuperHero type, and the compiler did not complain, the answer is the smart casting feature of the Kotlin compiler. Whenever you check in an `if` or a `when` statement that a type can be cast to another type, the compiler then allows you to access all members from the target type, that is, the compiler does the cast for you. Let's say we have a class hierarchy like the following one:

```
open class BaseUser(val name: String)

open class User(name: String,
                val birthYear: Int) : BaseUser(name) {
    fun login() {
    }
}
open class AdminUser(name: String,
                     birthYear: Int) : User(name, birthYear) {
    fun accessLogs() {
    }
}
```

We have a function that accepts the base type; we can check with the `is` keyword whether a type is an instance of another type. When the compiler knows that a type is actually an instance of a different type, you can immediately access all the members without casting:

```
fun smartCasting(baseUser: BaseUser) {
    if (baseUser is User) {
        baseUser.login()
    } else if (baseUser is AdminUser) {
        baseUser.accessLogs()
    }
}
```

Smart casting has some rules that need to be satisfied. The compiler has to be sure that a variable will not change after the instance of check. This rules out mutable fields and properties (`var` properties). The compiler cannot ensure that after a successful instance check, some other thread didn't modify it. This leaves smart casting usable by immutable properties (`val` properties) and local variables that are not accessed inside a closure (modified by a lambda function or an anonymous object).

Summary

After this chapter, you should have a good grasp of the object-oriented features of the Kotlin language. You should be comfortable with using classes, inheriting from them, and implementing interfaces. And if you have experience with some other OO languages, then you'll probably appreciate how Kotlin is less verbose and more readable than some of its competitors thanks to features such as data classes, primary constructors with properties, and class delegation.

In the next chapter, we will learn more about functions and see that they are first-class citizens in Kotlin.

4

Functions and Lambdas

This chapter is dedicated to functions. First, we'll see some more advanced features of functions in Kotlin that we've not covered in Chapter 2, *Kotlin Basics*. Then, the rest of the chapter is dedicated to function types and lambdas. Lambdas and function types are an essential part of Kotlin, and the standard library relies on and uses them extensively.

In this chapter, we will cover the following:

- Advanced functions
- Lambdas
- Function types

Advanced functions

We already covered the basics of functions in the next chapter. In this section, we'll cover additional features related to functions that are not present in Java, such as named arguments and default parameters.

Named arguments

Kotlin supports naming arguments when passing them to functions. This can make your code more verbose but can improve its readability.

Java doesn't have named function arguments, and the common approach in Java is to use the builder pattern when your class or function accepts multiple arguments. This makes the code even more verbose. Consider this regionMatches function call on the String type; it accepts five arguments and three of them are of the Int type:

```
String str = "foo";
boolean match = str.regionMatches(true, 0, "foo", 0, 3);
```

If you were reading this code for the first time, you'd probably have to look up this function documentation to see what all the arguments represent.

In Kotlin, thanks to named arguments, we can call the same function like this:

```
val str = "foo"
val match = str.regionMatches(thisOffset = 0, other = "foo", otherOffset =
0, length = 3, ignoreCase = true)
```

Now, we know what each argument represents without looking into the documentation of the Java standard library.

Another benefit of named arguments is that it makes your code less error-prone. Multiple arguments of the same type could easily be mistaken. With named arguments, this cannot happen.

If you use named arguments when calling a function, then you can place the arguments in any order you wish.

Also, when calling a function and using named arguments, you have to name all the arguments after the first named argument. This example names only one argument, `otherOffset`, without naming arguments that follow, and the compiler will not allow this:

```
val str = "foo"
//compiler error
val match = str.regionMatches(3, "foo", otherOffset = 0, 3, true)
```

But, this example compiles because all arguments after the first named one are also named:

```
val str = "foo"
val match = str.regionMatches(3, "foo", otherOffset = 0, length = 3,
ignoreCase = true)
```

Named arguments can also be used on class constructors. If we have a class declaration like this:

```
class User(private val firstName: String,
           private val lastName: String,
           private val birthYear: Int)
```

We can then reverse the order of arguments when calling the constructor if we wish, as you can see here:

```
val user = User(birthYear = 1955, lastName = "Wayne", firstName = "Bruce")
```

Finally, since Java doesn't have named arguments, they can be only used when calling functions defined in Kotlin. Saving parameter names in the Java bytecode is possible from Java 8 and Kotlin has backward compatibility to Java 6. If you are wondering how we were able to use named arguments on a function that is defined on the string type in the Java standard library that is because this function was actually declared in the Kotlin standard library. The Kotlin standard library has numerous extension functions (we'll learn about them in the next chapter) that extend types from the Java standard library.

Default parameters

If you have experience with Java, then you probably have seen a class with multiple overloaded methods, or a class with multiple constructors that differ in a parameter count to provide better usability to users. `String` or `Thread` classes from the Java standard library are good examples of this. The problem is that, a lot of code has to be duplicated, and if you are writing a library, you'll probably want to have Java documents on each method, which again have to be duplicated.

Let's take a look at an example from the Java standard library. The `String` class has overloaded `indexOf` methods; this one accepts two integers as arguments. The first one is the Unicode character representation, and the second one is the index to start the search from:

```
public int indexOf(int ch, int fromIndex) {
    //omitted
}
```

Then, there is another overload of this method, which just calls the first one and provides a default argument for the start of a search index:

```
public int indexOf(int ch) {
    return indexOf(ch, 0);
}
```

Thanks to default parameter values, if this function was defined in Kotlin, no overloads would be needed. When defining a function parameter, you can also assign it a default value. This is how it would look in Kotlin:

```
fun indexOf(ch: Int, fromIndex: Int = 0) {
    //omitted
}
```

And when calling this function, you won't have to provide arguments that don't have a default value:

```
indexOf(65)
```

Of course, you can override the default argument value with your own:

```
indexOf(65, 1)
```

Default argument values are really useful when combined with named arguments. This gives you the option to specify arguments in any order you wish and omit ones that have default values.

Default argument values can also be used in class constructors. This User class has three constructors:

```
class User {

    constructor(name: String) : this(name, null)

    constructor(name:String,
                phoneNumber: String?) : this(name, phoneNumber, false)

    constructor(name:String,
                phoneNumber: String?,
                isLoggedIn: Boolean) {
        //omitted
    }
}
```

We can simplify this and have only one constructor:

```
class User(name: String,
           phoneNumber: String? = null,
           isLoggedIn: Boolean = false)
```

Since Java doesn't have default argument values, they can only be used in functions defined in Kotlin. If you plan on exposing your code to Java, Kotlin provides the @JvmOverloads annotation, which instructs the Kotlin compiler to produce overloaded methods for each default argument value. If we had this factory function:

```
@JvmOverloads
fun createUser(name: String, phoneNumber: String = "", loggedIn: Boolean =
false) : User {
    return User(name, phoneNumber, loggedIn)
}
```

The compiler would then produce the following overloads and the code would look like this in Java:

```
public static final User createUser(@NotNull String name)

public static final User createUser(@NotNull String name, @NotNull String
phoneNumber)

public static final User createUser(@NotNull String name, @NotNull String
phoneNumber, boolean loggedIn)
```

Variable function arguments

Variable function arguments are a feature that allows you to pass multiple argument values to a single function argument. This feature is also available in Java, and a function that accepts variable function arguments has three dots after the parameter type, like this:

```
public int sumNumbers(int... nums)
```

In Kotlin, you can have the same functionality if you apply the `vararg` keyword before a parameter name:

```
fun sumNumbers(vararg num: Int): Int {
    var result = 0
    for (i in num) {
        result += i
    }
    return result
}
```

Now, we can call this function and supply an arbitrary number of arguments to it:

```
val result = sumNumbers(1, 2, 3, 4, 5)
```

When calling a function with variable arguments, the compiler packs them into an array. What happens when you create an array yourself and want to pass it to a function with Varargs? This is where Kotlin differs from Java. Java lets you pass the array directly as an argument, but Kotlin doesn't. Kotlin requires that an array is explicitly unpacked. This is the responsibility of the spread operator, `*`. The next example shows how you'd call the previous function when unpacking the array:

```
val nums = intArrayOf(1, 2, 3, 4, 5)
val result = sumNumbers(*nums)
```

Lambdas

We've already seen how Kotlin can use the object keyword to create an anonymous instance of a class. This can be used when we want to pass some functionality as an argument to another method. But if the interface or a class you are creating has only one function, then using anonymous classes may feel cumbersome and too verbose.

This is where lambda expressions, or lambdas for short, come into play. Lambdas can be best described as short pieces of code that can be passed to other functions. If you have a Java background, then you probably remember how Java 8 was highly anticipated because it finally brought support for lambdas.

In UI programming, event listeners are the perfect use case for lambdas. We're going to take a look at an example from Android. Android still uses Java 6, and there we can't use Java lambdas, so it will be perfect to show how using Kotlin instead of Java is less verbose if you can't use the latest Java versions. On android with Java, you would set a click listener on a button object like this:

```java
public void setClickListener() {
    button.setOnClickListener(new View.OnClickListener() {
        @Override
        public void onClick(View v) {
            System.out.print("Clicked on: " + v.toString());
        }
    });
}
```

All view classes in android have the `setOnClickListener` method (which they inherit from the `View` base class), which accepts as an argument an instance of the `View.OnClickListener` interface. Most of the time, you'd pass this argument by creating an instance with an anonymous class on the fly, like we did in the previous example.

The same code in Kotlin, thanks to lambdas, can be expressed with one line only:

```kotlin
button.setOnClickListener({ v: View -> println("Clicked on: $v") })
```

Now, let's take a look at the code of the `View.OnClickListener` interface from the android source code, as it will help us with explaining the lambda syntax:

```java
/**
 * Interface definition for a callback to be invoked when a view is
clicked.
 */
public interface OnClickListener
```

```
{
    /**
     * Called when a view has been clicked.
     *
     * @param v The view that was clicked.
     */
    void onClick(View v);
}
```

The interface has only one method, `onClick`, and this is the method we've declared with the Kotlin lambda.

Lambda functions in Kotlin are always declared inside the curly braces. Inside the curly braces, first we declare the parameters of our lambda; our `onClick` method accepts one, a `View` type. If there were more, they'd be separated by commas. Note that parameters are not enclosed inside parentheses.

After the parameters comes the arrow (`->`) and then the lambda body. You can think of this arrow as trying to say that parameters from the left are passed to the body on the right.

Type inference also works on lambda parameters; you don't have to explicitly specify that the `v` parameter is of `View` type:

```
button.setOnClickListener { v -> println("Clicked on: $v") }
```

Lambdas don't have to be one-liners like the previous example. You can also declare them with multiple lines inside the body. Here's how we would define a lambda that sums two integers with a multiline body:

```
{
    a: Int, b: Int ->
        println("Summing numbers: $a and $b")
        val result = a + b
        println("The result is: $result")
        result
}
```

Returning a value from a lambda

The previous click listener lambda had no return type. But, what if your lambda needs to return a value? Let's write a lambda that returns a sum of two integers that are passed as arguments:

```
{ a: Int, b: Int -> a + b }
```

You probably noticed that there is no `return` keyword. In fact, if we declared a `return` keyword, we'd get a compiler error stating that return is not allowed there:

```
// compiler error
{ a: Int, b: Int -> return a + b }
```

The return keyword is not allowed and Kotlin implicitly considers the last line of a lambda as a return expression. Of course, only if the lambda signature states that there should be a return value. In a `void` method, like the click listener example from the beginning, the last line is not considered as a return expression.

Passing lambdas as the only or last argument

When a lambda is passed to a function as the only or last argument, enclosing it in parentheses is optional. Let's go back to our click listener example. We could have also written it like this:

```
button.setOnClickListener { v -> println("Clicked on: $v") }
```

This feature enhances readability and is particularly useful if you are creating a **DSL** (**Domain-Specific Language**) with Kotlin.

Closures

If you are not familiar with the concept of a closure, the easiest way to describe it would be as a scope (function) that can access the state (variables) of another scope. When you define local variables inside a function, then their scope is the body of that function. A function can also declare a lambda expression, which has its own scope. You can access local variables of the outer function from the lambda expression. This is a closure.

Java also supports a closure with anonymous classes and lambdas. But, there is one big difference between Kotlin and Java. When Java closes over a variable, it captures its value. That's why you can only close over variables that have the final modifier, that is, they are immutable.

The following example tries to modify a local variable from an anonymous class, but the compiler will throw an error here because the local variable is not final:

```
int a = 0;
Runnable runnable = new Runnable()
{
    @Override
```

```
public void run() {
    a++; //compiler error
}
};
```

But, if you put the final modifier into a variable, then you won't be able to modify it. So, the trick is to wrap the variable inside a final one-sized array or the `AtomicReference` type:

```
final int[] a = { 0 };
Runnable runnable = new Runnable() {
    @Override
    public void run() {
        a[0]++;
    }
};
```

In Kotlin, there are no restrictions like in Java. You can access non-final variables inside a closure and also modify them. Similar code in Kotlin shows this:

```
var a = 0
val closure = {
    a++
}
```

Returning from lambdas

Let's imagine that you have a lambda function and you want to exit from it early, like in this example:

```
fun returnStatement() {
    val nums = arrayOf(1, 2, 3, 4, 5)
    println("Started iterating the array")
    nums.forEach { n ->
        if (n > 2) {
            return
        }
    }
    println("Finished iterating the array")
}
```

This code will never print Finished iterating the array. The reason is that the return statement inside the lambda is a non-local return, and it returns from the top-level block and not the block where it is declared. If you think that doesn't make sense, if you use the return statement inside a for statement or a while loop, it would also exit the top-level block, not the loop itself.

Kotlin allows return statements to have labels. You can define your own you label or use the default one, which is the function name. This is how we can fix the previous example to print the last statement with the default return label:

```
fun returnStatement() {
    val nums = arrayOf(1, 2, 3, 4, 5)
    println("Started iterating the array")
    nums.forEach { n ->
        if (n > 2) {
            return@forEach
        }
    }
    println("Finished iterating the array")
}
```

Here's how you would define your own label. Before the lambda block, place the name of your label followed by the @ character:

```
fun returnStatement() {
    val lamdba = label@ {
        return@label
    }
}
```

Function types

Functions are first-class citizens in Kotlin. You can define function types and store them in variables. Functions can return other functions and accept functions as arguments.

Defining function types

Let's take a look at an example of how to define a function type and initialize the variable with a lambda:

```
val multiplier: (Int, Int) -> Int = { a, b -> a * b }
```

This function type has two parameters of type `Int` and returns an `Int`. The function type syntax always starts with parentheses, where you declare function parameters, then the arrow, and after the arrow, a return type.

Here's how you'd declare a function type that has no parameters and no return type:

```
val print: () -> Unit = { println("Kotlin") }
```

Of course, type inference works on function types, so the preceding example could have been written like this:

```
val print2 = { println("Kotlin") }
```

Function types can also be nullable; notice how we need to wrap the whole function type inside another set of parentheses and then place a question mark:

```
val nullableFun: (() -> Unit)? = null
```

Without them, it would mean that the return type of a function type is nullable, like in this example:

```
val nullableReturnType: () -> String? = { null }
```

Calling function types

Now that you know how to define a function type, let's see how we can make use of them.

Calling a function type is the same as calling a normal function. You put parentheses after the function variable or the argument that is a function type. Here's a function that simulates a long-running task and accepts two callback functions, one in the case of successful completion and one in the case of an error. Inside the function, you can see how we call the onFinished and onError function type arguments:

```
fun longRunningTask(onFinished: (Any) -> Unit, onError: (Throwable) ->
Unit) {
    try {
        //something long running
        onFinished("got result")
    } catch (fail: Throwable) {
        onError(fail)
    }
}
```

All function types also have the invoke method (we'll see in the *Calling function types from Java* section why this is), which can also be used to call a function type, like this example shows:

```
fun longRunningTask(onFinished: (result: Any) -> Unit, onError: (fail:
Throwable) -> Unit) {
    try {
        //something long running
        onFinished.invoke("got result")
    } catch (fail: Throwable)
```

```
    {
        onError.invoke(fail)
    }
}
```

Naming parameters of function types

So far, we've defined all our function type parameters without names. Kotlin allows function type parameters to have names. Let's go back to our long-running task example and show how we can name the parameters:

```
fun longRunningTask(onFinished: (result: Any) -> Unit, onError: (fail:
Throwable) -> Unit)
```

The benefit of this is code completion inside the IDE. But, this doesn't force you to name your lambda arguments like this. You can then call the function with the parameter names from the function type:

```
longRunningTask({ result -> println("Result: $result") }, { fail ->
println("Error: ${fail.message}") })
```

Or, you can use your own names, as you can see here:

```
longRunningTask({ r -> println("Result: $r") }, { err -> println("Error:
${err.message}") })
```

Calling function types from Java

Java doesn't have function types; instead, it uses interfaces with a single method or functional interfaces to achieve similar behavior. Kotlin compiles its function types to functional interfaces, called Function0, Function1, Function2, and so on. The number at the end represents the number of function parameters. Here is how they are defined in the Kotlin standard library. Don't worry about the angle brackets or in and out keywords; these are generic functions. We'll learn about generics in the following chapters:

```
/** A function that takes 0 arguments. */
public interface Function0<out R> : Function<R> {
    /** Invokes the function. */
    public operator fun invoke(): R
}
/** A function that takes 1 argument. */
public interface Function1<in P1, out R> : Function<R> {
    /** Invokes the function with the specified argument. */
    public operator fun invoke(p1: P1): R
```

```
    }
    /** A function that takes 2 arguments. */
    public interface Function2<in P1, in P2, out R> : Function<R> {
        /** Invokes the function with the specified arguments. */
        public operator fun invoke(p1: P1, p2: P2): R
    }
```

All interfaces have a single method called `invoke`. This is why you can call function types either as you would call a normal function, with the parentheses at the end, or by calling the `invoke` function of the interface.

Since function types get compiled to interfaces, you can call them from Java. If the Java version you are running supports lambdas, they will be converted to Kotlin function types automatically. Let's suppose that we have a function in Kotlin that accepts a function type as an argument:

```
fun applyLambda(a: Int, b: Int, modifierFunc: (Int, Int) -> Int) {
    val result = modifierFunc(a, b)
    println("Result of applying a function: $result")
}
```

Calling it from Java with a lambda would look like this. The Kotlin function is defined in a file called `KotlinFunctionTypes`. That is why we call it from the compiler generated `KotlinFunctionTypesKt` class:

```
KotlinFunctionTypesKt.applyLambda(10, 2, (a, b) -> a * b);
```

And if your Java version doesn't support lambdas, you can also use anonymous classes:

```
KotlinFunctionTypesKt.applyLambda(10, 2, new Function2<Integer, Integer,
Integer>() {
    @Override
    public Integer invoke(Integer a, Integer b) {
        return a * b;
    }
});
```

Lambdas and SAM types

Java has numerous functional interfaces that have only one method. They are called **SAM** types, which stands for **Single Abstract Method**. One example of that kind of interface is `IntPredicate` from the Java standard library:

```
@FunctionalInterface
public interface IntPredicate {
```

```
/**
 * Evaluates this predicate on the given argument.
 *
 * @param value the input argument
 * @return {@code true} if the input argument matches the predicate,
 * otherwise {@code false}
 */
boolean test(int value);
}
```

In the next example, we are trying to create this interface with a lambda, but the compiler will throw an error:

```
fun createPredicate(): IntPredicate {
    //compiler error
    return  { n: Int -> n % 2 == 0 }
}
```

Even though the function signature of the interface and the lambda match—they both accept an `int` as the parameter and return a `Boolean`—the compiler is complaining because in the lambda return statement, it sees a function type of `Function1` but `IntPredicate` is needed.

To make it compile, we have to put the name of the interface before the lambda expression, similar to casting a type but without parentheses:

```
fun createPredicate(): IntPredicate {
    return  IntPredicate { n -> n % 2 == 0 }
}
```

Member references

If you already have a member function that you'd like to assign to a function type, you could wrap it inside a lambda:

```
var numFunc: (Int, Int) -> Int = { a, b -> multiplier(a, b) }

fun multiplier(a: Int, b: Int): Int {
    return a * b
}
```

You can also initialize the function type directly with a member reference, the same as you can in Java 8:

```
var numFunc: (Int, Int) -> Int = this::multiplier

fun multiplier(a: Int, b: Int): Int {
    return a * b
}
```

Member references are expressed with the `::` operator. On the left-hand side of the operator is the object that holds the function. We use `this` since we are referring to the same object that holds the `numFunc` function type property. On the right-hand side is the function name.

When the function is declared in the same class or the same file as the function type variable, you can omit the `this` from the left-hand side of the `::` operator. We can also write it like this:

```
var numFunc: (Int, Int) -> Int = ::multiplier
```

The member function has to have the same signature as the function type that is being initialized; otherwise, you'd get a compiler error:

```
//compiler error
var numFunc: (Int, Int) -> Int = this::printNums

fun printNums(a: Int, b: Int) {
    println("$a and $b")
}
```

And if you want to use a function from some other object to initialize a function type variable, you just have to set the name of the object variable on the left-hand side of the `::` operator, as the following example shows:

```
val str = "Kotlin"
val getChar: (Int) -> Char = str::get
```

Member references can also be used to get a reference to a class constructor. Constructors are also functions, so we can store a reference to it and invoke it later. The syntax for targeting a class constructor looks like this; it's just the class name after the `::` operator:

```
class Person(val name: String)
val personConstructor = ::Person
```

Now, we can invoke a person constructor function type and we'll get an instance of the `Person` type:

```
val person: Person = personConstructor("John")
```

Inlining lambdas

Calling a function always incurs a slight (negligible in most cases) overhead, no matter what kind of programming language you use. And in the case of Kotlin and function types, there is also the overhead of allocating memory on the heap, since function types are objects.

To avoid this overhead, Kotlin offers the `inline` keyword, which can be placed before the `fun` keyword when declaring a function. Inlining can be described as moving the functionality of a called function to its caller function.

To see the difference between inline and normal functions, let's declare functions with same body and signature, but one will be inlined:

```
fun noInline(func: () -> String) {
    val str = func()
    println("Func produced: $str")
}

inline fun inlined(func: () -> String) {
    val str = func()
    println("Func produced: $str")
}
```

And now, let's see what the compiler does with both of these functions. This is Java bytecode decompiled back to Java:

```
public static final void noInline(@NotNull Function0 func) {
    Intrinsics.checkParameterIsNotNull(func, "func");
    String str = (String)func.invoke();
    String var2 = "Func produced: " + str;
    System.out.println(var2);
}

public static final void inlined(@NotNull Function0 func) {
    Intrinsics.checkParameterIsNotNull(func, "func");
    String str = (String)func.invoke();
    String var3 = "Func produced: " + str;
    System.out.println(var3);
}
```

They get compiled exactly the same. But that's not a surprise; we are not calling the inline function, so there is nothing to inline. Let's now see the difference when we call each of them:

```
fun callInlined() {
    inlined { "Kotlin" }
}

fun callNotInlined() {
    noInline { "Kotlin" }
}
```

First, let's see the not-inlined function:

```
public static final void callNotInlined() {
    noInline((Function0)$callNotInlined$1.INSTANCE);
}
```

There is the function call and as an argument, an instance of the function type is provided. This instance comes from the extra class that the compiler generated, and it looks something like this:

```
public class $callNotInlined$1 extends kotlin.jvm.internal.Lambda
implements Function0<String> {

    private $callNotInlined$1() {
        super(0);
    }

    @Override
    public String invoke() {
        String str$iv = "Kotlin";
        return str$iv;
    }

    public static final $callNotInlined$1 INSTANCE;

    static {
        INSTANCE = new $callNotInlined$1();
    }
}
```

So, for the normal function call, without inlining, the compiler allocates an extra object on the heap and stores it to a static field, so the same instance of the function type is reused whenever this function type is needed.

Now, let's take a look at the bytecode output of the inlined function:

```
public static final void callInlined() {
    String str$iv = "Kotlin";
    String var1 = "Func produced: " + str$iv;
    System.out.println(var1);
}
```

The inlined function doesn't have the extra class or the extra function call. The compiler took the code from the lambda that represents our function type and placed that code directly into the call site, thus avoiding a function call and the creation of an additional object on the heap.

The inline keyword is also allowed on property accessor methods:

```
var str: String
    inline get() = "Kotlin"
    inline set(value) {
        println("$value passed as parameter")
    }
```

Also, only one property method can be inlined:

```
var str: String
    get() = "Kotlin"
    inline set(value) {
        println("$value passed as parameter")
    }
```

Or, the property itself can have the inline keyword, which then implies both get and set methods are inlined:

```
inline var str: String
    get() = "Kotlin"
    set(value) {
        println("$value passed as parameter")
    }
```

You can place the inline keyword even if your function doesn't accept a function type as a parameter:

```
inline fun nothingToInline() {

}
```

In this case, the compiler will generate a warning only, saying that the performance impact is negligible and that you should use inline only with function type parameters. This is a good warning and can be used as a guide for when to use the `inline` keyword. If you just want to avoid an additional function call, don't use inline; leave that optimization to the runtime. If your function accepts a function type parameter, then inlining can avoid creating an instance of both a class and a function call.

noinline

If your function accepts more than one function type parameter, and you don't want to inline all parameters, you can place the `noinline` keyword in front of the ones you don't want inlined. As the next example shows, the first function argument will be inlined and the second will not be:

```
inline fun noInlineExample(first: () -> String, noinline second: () ->
String) {
    //omitted
}
```

crossinline

When your inlined function calls a function type passed to it as a parameter from a different execution context than the body of the inline function, such as a nested function call, the compiler will not allow it because the function type may have a non-local control flow. In such cases, you can add the `crossinline` keyword to the function type parameter to tell the compiler that a non-local control flow is not allowed. The following example compiles because we have the `crossinline` keyword:

```
fun firstFunctionType(f: () -> String) {
    println(f.invoke())
}

inline fun secondFunctionType(crossinline f: () -> String) {
    firstFunctionType {
        f.invoke()
    }
}
```

If you remove the `crossinline` keyword, the compiler will throw an error.

Summary

In this chapter, we saw how named and default arguments can help when working with functions with multiple parameters. We also saw how Kotlin supports function types and how function types can be created with lambda expressions. They are an important part of the language and Kotlin relies heavily on them.

In the next chapter we'll be exploring more advanced features of Kotlin.

5
Advanced Kotlin

In this chapter, we'll cover various Kotlin features that are not related to each other, but could be classified as advanced. These are maybe not the features that you use daily, but nevertheless are worth knowing, because most of them are unique to Kotlin.

We'll learn about the following:

- Generics
- Concurrency constructs
- Delegated properties
- Extension functions
- Extension properties
- Receiver functions
- Infix functions
- Creating a DSL
- Operator overloading

Generics

We've already seen generics in previous chapters, and in this section, we'll learn how they work, how they are implemented, and what the differences are from generics in Java.

Simply put, generics are types with parameters. Take a look at the `List` interface, for example; without generics, you could add objects of any type to it. But, since the list interface is generic, you have to specify a generic type for when you are creating an instance of it. You can create a list of strings, a list of integers, and so on. This then makes the list type-safe; you cannot add an integer to a list of strings.

The generic type is specified in angle brackets, so a list of strings type is declared like this:

```
List<String>
```

Creating an instance of a generic type is the same as creating normal types; you call a generic class constructor and specify the generic type argument:

```
val strings: List<String> = ArrayList<String>()
```

Type inference works with generics also, so supplying the generic argument of string in the `ArrayList` class constructor is redundant. When a variable has declared a generic type, then you can omit it from the constructor:

```
val strings: List<String> = ArrayList()
```

Type inference also works on variables; if there is enough information from the variable declaration, you can omit the type:

```
val strings = ArrayList<String>()
```

Declaring generic types

You can declare a generic class or interface with angle brackets after the type name. In the angle brackets, you specify the name of your generic type parameter. Usually, generic types are called T or E.

Let's see how the generic `Array` class is declared in the Kotlin Standard Library:

```
public class Array<T> {

  public inline constructor(size: Int, init: (Int) -> T)

  public operator fun get(index: Int): T

  public operator fun set(index: Int, value: T): Unit

  public val size: Int

  public operator fun iterator(): Iterator<T>
}
```

Notice, how, in the generic type declaration, there is no information about the actual generic type argument. We only reserved a place for it and gave it a name, T. The actual generic type argument will be given at compile time.

You can see how, in the body of the class, we have access to the generic T type. For example, the `get` function returns the generic type. When you create an instance of, let's say, an array of strings, then this `get` function return type will be a string type.

Declaring a generic interface is done in the same way as with generic classes, with angle brackets after the type name:

```
interface Generic<T> {
    fun foo(t: T)
}
```

When implementing this interface, you have to specify a generic type. This class uses the `Int` type as the generic type:

```
class IntGeneric: Generic<Int> {
    override fun foo(t: Int) {

    }
}
```

You can see how the `foo` method's parameter also changes to the `Int` type.

We can also let the callers of our class decide upon the generic type. We do this by declaring the class itself to be generic:

```
class GenericType<T>: Generic<T> {
    override fun foo(t: T) {

    }
}
```

Notice how the `foo` method's parameter is again now of the generic T type.

Generic functions

We've seen how you can declare a function that accepts or returns a generic type inside a generic class. You can also have generic functions declared inside a non-generic type. Declaring a generic function is done with the angle brackets after the `fun` keyword:

```
class NonGeneric {

    fun <T> genericFunc(t: T) {
        println(t.toString())
    }
}
```

Calling the generic function is done by specifying the generic type in the angle brackets after the function name:

```
nonGeneric.genericFunc<String>("Kotlin")
```

Of course, if the compiler can infer the type passed to the function, you can omit specifying the type:

```
nonGeneric.genericFunc("Kotlin")
```

Generic constraints

Up to now, we could have substituted the generic parameter with any type. Sometimes, you may want to restrict the generic types and this can be done with generic constraints. Constraints are specified in angle brackets, with a colon, and the type that is the limit after the generic parameter. Here's how you can limit the generic type to the Number type:

```
interface Countable<T: Number>
{
    fun count(): T
}
```

This is known as the **upper bound** constraint, and the compiler will allow you to substitute the generic type with the Number type and all of its subtypes. Since the Int type is a subtype of the Number type, the compiler allows this:

```
class IntCountable: Countable<Int>
{
    override fun count(): Int
    {
        return 0
    }
}
```

But, the string type is not a subtype of Number, so the next example will not compile:

```
//compiler error
class StringCountable: Countable<String> {
    override fun count(): String {
        return ""
    }
}
```

Constraints can also be declared with the `where` keyword after the class or function declaration. The `Countable` interface could have also been declared like this:

```
interface Countable2<T> where T: Number {
    fun count(): T
}
```

You can also have multiple constraints on a single generic parameter. When more than one constraint is specified, they have to use the `where` keyword. You use a comma to separate all the constraints. This interface puts a constraint on a `Number` type and `Comparable` interface:

```
interface Countable3<T> where T: Number, T: Comparable<T> {
    fun count(): T
}
```

Constraints also work on generic functions; the syntax is the same as for declaring them on types.

Type erasure and raw types

Generics were introduced in Java version 1.5. To maintain backward compatibility, generics in Java are implemented with a concept known as **type erasure**. During compile time, in Java all generic type information is lost (erased). So, for example, the `Comparable<T>` interface gets compiled to `Comparable<Object>`; there are no generic parameters in the generated Java bytecode. The compiler is responsible for type checks and enforcing type safety. At runtime, you cannot know what the generic parameter was substituted with.

This is one of the reasons why Java has raw types. Raw types are generic types without type arguments. For example, `Comparable<T>` is a generic interface, and in Java you can declare this type without a generic type:

```
private Comparable comparable;
```

Kotlin compiles generics like Java, that is, it uses type erasure. But, Kotlin doesn't have backward compatibility issues since generics have been part of the language since the earliest versions. This is one of the reasons (type safety is another) why raw types are not allowed in Kotlin. The following example will not compile:

```
//compiler error
private lateinit var comparable: Comparable
```

Reified generics

In the previous section, we described how you cannot know what generic type arguments are used during runtime because of type erasure. The following code tries to get the class type of the generic argument, but will not compile because the runtime doesn't have information about the generic T type that will be used when invoking this function:

```
fun <T> createInstance(): T {

    //compiler error
    return T::class.java.newInstance()

}
```

Knowing generic type information can sometimes be useful and Kotlin can bypass this limitation with reified generics. A generic type can be reified with inline functions. We explained how inlining works in the previous chapter.

 When the compiler sees an inline function, it places the inlined function directly into the call site.

This is needed for reification to work since Kotlin has to produce Java compatible bytecode, so it has to erase the generic type information during compilation. The same as lambda inlining, the compiler knows which code is calling an inline marked function, and in the case of generics, it knows which generic type argument is being used. The generic function will still go under type erasure but the bytecode will already have generic type information.

Now that we know the internals of reified generics, let's compile the previous example:

```
inline fun <reified T> createReifiedInstance():T {

    return T::class.java.newInstance()

}
```

Besides the required `inline` keyword, you have to add the `reified` keyword before the generic parameter. And then, inside the function, we can access the generic type as if there was no type erasure.

Concurrency constructs

If you ever wrote concurrent code in Java, you probably used some of its concurrency primitives. It might surprise you that Kotlin doesn't have any constructs for dealing with concurrency as part of the language. The Kotlin design team felt that this should be the job of libraries. The Kotlin standard library has, in the base `kotlin` package and the `kotlin.concurrent` package, several functions, and annotations that can compile to Java's concurrency primitives.

Concurrent programming is a huge topic and we could write an entire book about it. So in this section, we'll cover only what Kotlin has to offer for concurrent programming.

Starting a thread

Doing some work in a different thread can be done in Kotlin the same as in Java, by creating an instance of the `Thread` class with a `Runnable` function and then starting it. Kotlin also offers a shortcut function called `thread` that is a little bit easier to use. It has several default parameters and only needs a lambda that will be executed in the newly created thread:

```
thread {
    //something long running
    println("Work done")
}
```

This is how the `thread` function is defined in the standard library:

```
/**
 * Creates a thread that runs the specified [block] of code.
 *
 * @param start if 'true', the thread is immediately started.
 * @param isDaemon if 'true', the thread is created as a daemon thread. The
Java Virtual Machine exits when
 * the only threads running are all daemon threads.
 * @param contextClassLoader the class loader to use for loading classes
and resources in this thread.
 * @param name the name of the thread.
 * @param priority the priority of the thread.
 */
public fun thread(
    start: Boolean = true,
    isDaemon: Boolean = false,
    contextClassLoader: ClassLoader? = null,
    name: String? = null,
```

```
    priority: Int = -1,
    block: () -> Unit
): Thread
```

If you are interested in just offloading some work to a background thread, then almost all of these parameters can be left with their default values.

Synchronized methods

Java has the `synchronized` keyword, which can be applied to methods to ensure that only one thread at a time can access them. A thread that enters a synchronized method obtains a lock (an object being locked is the instance of the containing class) and no other thread can enter the method until the lock is released. Kotlin offers the same functionality with the `@Synchronized` annotation. When applied to a method, it will produce the same bytecode as Java would with the `synchronized` keyword:

```
@Synchronized
fun threadSafeFunction() {

}
```

Synchronized blocks

Sometimes, holding a lock for the entire duration of a function call is too expensive and Java offers to run parts of the code under a lock, again with the `synchronized` keyword. To achieve the same behavior, Kotlin offers the `synchronized` function. The function accepts an object that will be locked and a lambda to execute while holding the lock:

```
fun synchronizedBlock() {
    // multiple threads can be here
    synchronized(this) {
        //only one thread at a time can be here
    }
}
```

Volatile

Java also offers the `volatile` keyword, which when applied to a field of a class instructs the CPU to always read it from the RAM and not from the CPU cache. It also prevents instructions reordering; it acts as a memory barrier. The same as with the `synchronized` methods, in Kotlin you apply the annotation to a property to have the same effect as Java's `volatile` keyword:

```
@Volatile
private var counter = 0
```

But be careful with this construct, as often it is not enough to achieve thread safety. For example, if we have a method that increments this field and more than one thread accesses this method, it could lead to unpredictable results. Incrementing an integer consists of more than one action: first, a variable has to be read from the memory, then it can be incremented and written back to the memory. To achieve thread safety, these actions have to be atomic, and volatile doesn't have that guarantee. So, if you are not familiar with the details of the Java memory model, it is better to use synchronized blocks. Uncontended locks have a negligible performance impact and are a lot harder to get wrong.

Delegated properties

We've already seen previously in `Chapter 3`, *Classes and Object-Oriented Programming*, about classes how Kotlin's `by` keyword can be used for class delegation. The same keyword can also be used for property delegation. As the name suggests, this concept allows a property's `get` or `set` methods to be delegated to another object. First, we'll learn how to write a delegate, then we'll see what delegates are included with the standard library.

Let's say we want a property that is lazily initialized, that is, initialized when accessed for the first time. We can use a delegate property for this:

```
private val str by lazyProperty { "I'm lazily initialized" }
```

The syntax for a delegate property is the `by` keyword, followed by an expression that returns an instance of the `ReadOnlyProperty` interface in the case of an immutable property, or the `ReadWriteProperty` interface in the case of a mutable property. This is how the interfaces are defined:

```
public interface ReadOnlyProperty<in R, out T> {
    public operator fun getValue(thisRef: R, property: KProperty<*>): T
}
```

The `ReadWriteProperty` interface also has a setter method:

```
public interface ReadWriteProperty<in R, T> {
    public operator fun getValue(thisRef: R, property: KProperty<*>): T
    public operator fun setValue(thisRef: R, property: KProperty<*>, value:
T)
}
```

Now, let's create a class that implements `ReadOnlyProperty`, which enables lazy initialization. Please note that this version is not thread safe. The standard library already ships with a thread safe delegate for lazy initialization, as we shall see later:

```
class LazyProperty<T>(private val valueFactory: () -> T) :
ReadOnlyProperty<Any, T> {
    private var instance: T? = null

    override fun getValue(thisRef: Any, property: KProperty<*>): T {
        if (instance == null) {
            instance = valueFactory()
        }
        return instance!!
    }
}
```

The interfaces have two generic parameters: the first one represents the type that will own the property, and the second the type of the property itself. In our case, we set the first generic argument to `Any`, which means that there are no restrictions on types that can host our delegated property. The second parameter is left as generic, which means that there are no restrictions on the property type itself and that the actual type will be determined at compile time.

`getValue` is a method that enables the delegated property; it states how the delegate provides the property value.

Delegates of mutable properties have to implement the `ReadWriteProperty` interface, and there you have one additional method, `setValue`, which states how the properties value is written.

Standard library delegate properties

Now that we know how to write a custom delegate property, we'll see what properties ship with the Kotlin standard library.

lazy

We wrote a version of a lazily initialized property in the previous section. The standard library has a better version of a delegate property for delaying object creation. An instance of the lazy interface is produced with the `lazy` function:

```
val str by lazy { "I'm lazily initialized" }
```

The lazy function can accept also a `LazyThreadSafetyMode` enum, which has three values:

- If you don't specify a value from this enum, `SYNCHRONIZED` will be used. This is a thread-safe mode and uses synchronization for thread safety.
- The `PUBLICATION` mode can be accessed by multiple concurrent callers, but the value from the first accessor will be returned.
- The `NONE` mode is not thread safe and should be used only when you are sure that only one thread will be accessing the delegate property.

The following code includes the preceding three values:

```
public enum class LazyThreadSafetyMode {

    /**
     * Locks are used to ensure that only a single thread can initialize
the [Lazy] instance.
     */
    SYNCHRONIZED,

    /**
     * Initializer function can be called several times on concurrent
access to uninitialized [Lazy] instance value,
     * but only the first returned value will be used as the value of
[Lazy] instance.
     */
    PUBLICATION,

    /**
     * No locks are used to synchronize an access to the [Lazy] instance
value; if the instance is accessed from multiple threads, its behavior is
```

```
undefined.
 *
 * This mode should not be used unless the [Lazy] instance is
guaranteed never to be initialized from more than one thread.
 */
 NONE,
}
```

observable

The `observable` function gives you a delegate property that accepts a function that will be invoked each time a property changes:

```
var observable by Delegates.observable(1) { prop, oldVal, newVal ->
    println("Observable property changed from $oldVal to $newVal")
}
```

If we now change the property, the lambda function will be invoked:

```
//this prints Observable property changed from 1 to 0
observable = 0
```

vetoable

This one is similar to observable; it accepts a function that will be invoked before each change of a property. But, `vetoable` can block the change, the function passed returns a `Boolean`, and if `false` is returned, the attempted change will be discarded and the property will have its old value. Let's say we have an `Int` property and allow only numbers less than `10`:

```
var vetoable by Delegates.vetoable(1) { prop, oldVal, newVal ->
    return@vetoable newVal <= 10
}
```

If we now try to assign `100` to it, the change will be blocked:

```
//change is blocked
vetoable = 100
```

And if the lambda returns `true`, the change will be successful:

```
//changed to 0
vetoable = 0
```

notNull

This delegate property is similar to lateinit properties. It allows a property to be declared without an initial value. If the value hasn't been set yet and you try to read it, an exception is thrown:

```
var notNull by Delegates.notNull<Int>()
```

The value hasn't been set yet and if we try to read it, an exception will be thrown:

```
//this results in exception
val n = notNull
```

We have to assign a value to the property first:

```
notNull = 1
val num = notNull
```

Extension functions

Often, you can encounter a situation where you wish you could add some functionality to a type that you don't own. This is what extension functions enable you to do. This is a concept where you can add members (functions and properties) to a type, outside of its definition, but still call it as a normal member. Here is one such example; we'll extend the Int type and add a function that checks if it is a power of two:

```
fun Int.isPowerOf2(): Boolean {
    return this > 0 && ((this and this - 1) == 0)
}
```

The syntax of an extension function is similar to normal functions, you just add the type that you are extending followed by the dot before the function name.

We can call the function now as a normal member:

```
val n = 8
val isPowerOf2 = n.isPowerOf2()
```

Inside the extension function, this keyword refers to the instance of the type we've extended. In our example, this keyword inside the extension function would refer to number eight.

Note that inside the extension function, you cannot access private members of the type you are extending.

Importing extension functions

Just as with any other type, extension functions have to be imported if they won't be used. Our isPowerOf2 extension is defined in the quickstart.kotlin.extensions package, so we'd import it in the file where we want to use it:

```
import quickstart.kotlin.extensions.isPowerOf2
```

Java interoperability

Kotlin compiles extension functions as static functions that accept the type being extended as the first argument. This makes it possible to use them from Java. Our isPowerOf2 extension function is defined in a file named ExtensionFunctions, and calling the function from Java would look like this:

```
int n = 8;

boolean isPowerOf2 = ExtensionFunctionsKt.isPowerOf2(n);
```

Extension properties

Kotlin also offers adding properties to existing types with extension properties. Just as extension functions have the type they are extending before a function name, extension properties are like normal properties with the addition of the extended type before the property name. The function we wrote in the previous section can also be written as a property:

```
val Int.isPowerOf2: Boolean

    get() = this > 0 && ((this and this - 1) == 0)
```

Now, we can access this property on any variable of Int type:

```
val n = 16

val isPowerOf2 = n.isPowerOf2
```

You can also have a mutable extension property, where you'd have to implement the set method also.

Receiver functions

Kotlin has built-in language features for creating custom DSLs. Receiver functions and the `Infix` keyword (covered in the next section) are two of those features.

Although intended primarily for creating DSLs, receiver functions can be also useful in everyday programming and as we shall see later, the Kotlin standard library uses them in several utility functions.

We could say that receiver functions share some similarities with extension functions. They have the same syntax for marking the receiver and, inside the function, they can access members of the receiver instance. Here's how we'd define a receiver function type:

```
val hello: String.() -> Unit = { print("Hello $this") }
```

It's the same as a normal function type definition, with the addition of the receiver type and a dot before the function signature.

To call this function, we have to provide an instance of the receiver type, a string in our case:

```
hello("Kotlin") // prints Hello Kotlin
```

You can see how, inside the receiver function body, we have access to the instance of the receiver type with this keyword.

Now, let's see an example that shows a more real-world usage scenario. Let's write a function for building a string; it accepts a receiver function with `StringBuilder` as the receiver type:

```
fun buildString(init: StringBuilder.() -> Unit): String {
    val builder = StringBuilder()
    init(builder)
    return builder.toString()
}
```

We create the `StringBuilder` instance inside the function, apply the receiver function to it, and then build the resultant string. This enables us to create a string object like this:

```
val string = buildString {
    append("Hello Receiver Functions")
    appendln("We have access to StringBuilder object inside this lambda")
}
```

Notice how, inside the lambda, we are accessing members of the `StringBuilder` type.

Infix functions

This is another feature of Kotlin that is intended for creating DSLs. Infix functions are like normal functions, but they can be called without the dot and parentheses. To declare an infix function, you have to place the `infix` keyword before the `fun` keyword. Here's an example:

```
class Employee {
    infix fun payout(salary: Int) {
        print("Employee was paid: $salary")
    }
}
```

Now, we can call the `payout` function without the dot and parentheses:

```
val employee = Employee()
employee payout 3500
```

These conditions have to be satisfied to use the `infix` keyword:

- Function has to have a single parameter
- Function has to be a member function or an extension function
- Parameters cannot be variable arguments
- Parameters cannot have a default value

Building a simple DSL

We can now put to use what we learned about receiver and infix functions and create a DSL for validating objects. To keep it simple, we'll only be validating `Int` types.

First, we'll add the `NumberValidator` interface. This is where all the different validators can represent their validation logic:

```
interface NumberValidator
{

    fun isValueValid(value: Int): Boolean

}
```

Then, we need a type that will keep all the validators and the validated object. We'll name it `Validator`:

```
class Validator<T> private constructor(private val validatedObject: T) {

    internal val validators = mutableListOf<NumberValidator>()
    private lateinit var valueFactory: (T) -> Int
}
```

To enforce type safety, the `Validator` type is generic. It has a list of validators and also holds a function type called `valueFactory`, which knows how to return a property that will be validated. Notice how the constructor is private. We don't allow the validator type to be created from outside; instead, we use an infix function that returns `Validator` instances:

```
companion object {
    infix fun <T> validates(obj: T): Validator<T> {
        return Validator(obj)
    }
}
```

The `Validator` type also needs a function to check all validation rules have been satisfied:

```
fun isValid(): Boolean {
    return validators.all { v ->
v.isValueValid(valueFactory(validatedObject)) }
}
```

And, we need a function that will initiate setting validation rules and choosing a property that will be validated:

```
infix fun forProperty(factory: (T) -> Int): RuleBuilder<T> {
    valueFactory = factory
    return RuleBuilder(this)
}
```

The `forProperty` function accepts a lambda with one parameter; the generic `T` represents the validated object and returns an `Int`. The full-blown validator would probably return another generic type, but since we are trying to keep it simple, we can only validate integers.

It returns a `RuleBuilder` object, which is used for defining various validation rules:

```
class RuleBuilder<T> internal constructor(internal val validator: Validator<T>) {

    fun greaterThan(target: Int): RuleBuilder<T> {
```

```
        validator.validators.add(object : NumberValidator {
            override fun isValueValid(value: Int): Boolean {
                return value > target
            }
        })
        return this
    }

    fun lesserThan(target: Int): RuleBuilder<T> {
        validator.validators.add(object : NumberValidator {
            override fun isValueValid(value: Int): Boolean {
                return value < target
            }
        })
        return this
    }

    fun finishRules(): Validator<T> {
        return validator
    }
}
```

Again, to keep it simple, we offer only two validators, `lesserThan` and `greaterThan`. Since each function returns the `RuleBuilder` object, we can set multiple rules by chaining calls one after another. But, it'd also be nice to set all the rules in one function call, so let's add an extension function that accepts a receiver type, which will enable this:

```
infix fun <T> RuleBuilder<T>.withRules(init: RuleBuilder<T>.() -> Unit):
Validator<T> {
    init(this)
    return this.validator
}
```

That's it, our mini DSL is ready. Let's see it in action.

This is the type that we'll validate:

```
class Employee(val age: Int, val name: String)
```

And we'll use its age property for setting the validation rules:

```
val employee = Employee(35, "John Wayne")

val validator = Validator validates employee forProperty { e -> e.age }
withRules {
    lesserThan(60)
    greaterThan(18)
}
```

```
val isValid = validator.isValid()
```

Thanks to our DSL, setting the validation rules reads almost like a proper English sentence.

Operator overloading

Operator overloading is a mechanism where programming language operators are implemented in custom, user-defined types. Most of the operators in Kotlin are actually functions. If you define a function in your type named `plus`, then you can use the + operator with the instance of that type. This increases flexibility and allows you to have a type defined in Java, and then use operators instead of functions in Kotlin. Also, thanks to extension functions, this enables adding an operator to existing types that you don't own.

The following table shows how operators map to functions:

Operator	Function
a++	a.inc()
a--	a.dec()
a + b	a.plus(b)
a - b	a.minus(b)
a * b	a.times(b)
a / b	a.div(b)
a % b	a.rem(b)
a..b	a.rangeTo(b)
a in b	b.contains(a)
a[i]	a.get(i)
a[i] = b	a.set(i, b)
a += b	a.plusAssign(b)
a -= b	a.minusAssign(b)
a *= b	a.timesAssign(b)
a /= b	a.divAssign(b)
a %= b	a.remAssign(b)
a == b	a.equals(b)
a > b	a.compareTo(b) > 0
a < b	a.compareTo(b) < 0
a >= b	a.compareTo(b) >= 0
a <= b	a.compareTo(b) <= 0

Operator overloading can make the code easier to understand. Let's say that you have two instances of Java's `BigInteger` class. They represent numbers and it would make the code easier to understand if we used the + operator to sum them, instead of calling the `add` function.

Let's say we've defined a type that represents a length of something. To keep it simple, we have only one property that represents the value of the length. It seems natural to use the + operator to add two lengths, so we're going to overload that operator. We have to find the function name of that operator and implement it with the `operator` keyword:

```kotlin
class Length(val value: Double) {
    operator fun plus(other: Length): Length {
        return Length(this.value + other.value)
    }
}
```

Now, we can add two lengths with the + operator:

```kotlin
val l1 = Length(12.0)
val l2 = Length(23.5)

val sum = l1 + l2
```

Have you noticed how the plus function accepts an instance of another `Length` class? If we wanted to use the + operator with other types, we'd just have to implement another plus function that accepts that type. Let's now make it possible to call the + operator with doubles:

```kotlin
operator fun plus(double: Double): Length {
    return Length(this.value + double)
}
```

And now, we can use doubles with the + operator:

```kotlin
val l3 = Length(10.0)
val sum1 = l3 + 12.0
```

The return type of an operator function doesn't have to return the same type as the containing class. Here's how we can overload length and string to return another string:

```kotlin
operator fun plus(str: String): String {
    return "$value $str"
}
```

If we now pass a string to the + operator, we'll get a string as return type:

```kotlin
val str: String = l1 + "kilometers"
```

Overloading with extension functions

We already said how it would be better to use operators instead of functions when working with the `BigInteger` class. Operator overloading also works with extension functions, and this enables you to overload operators on types that are defined in other libraries.

Here's how the Kotlin standard library overloads the * operator:

```
public inline operator fun BigInteger.times(other: BigInteger): BigInteger
= this.multiply(other)
```

Operator overloading and Java

Java doesn't support any kind of operator overloading, but it is possible to use operators with types defined in Java. We already said that Kotlin operators are functions, and if the Kotlin compiler sees a correctly named function, it will allow a matching operator to be used.

Let's go back to our `Length` type and define it again in Java:

```
public class JavaLength {

  private final double value;

  public JavaLength(double value) {
  this.value = value;
  }

  public double getValue() {
  return value;
  }

  public JavaLength plus(JavaLength other) {
  return new JavaLength(this.value + other.getValue());
  }
}
```

The Kotlin compiler sees our `plus` function and allows us to use the + operator to add two length objects:

```
val javaL1 = JavaLength(12.0)
val javaL2 = JavaLength(7.5)

val javaSum = javaL1 + javaL2
```

Bitwise operations

Kotlin doesn't have operators for the bitwise manipulation of integers. Bitwise operations in Kotlin are done with functions. The following table shows all bitwise manipulation functions:

Function	Operation
shl(bits)	signed shift left (<< in Java)
shr(bits)	signed shift right (>> in Java)
ushr(bits)	unsigned shift right(>>> in Java)
and(bits)	bitwise and (& in Java)
or(bits)	bitwise or (| in Java)
xor(bits)	bitwise xor (^ in Java)
inv()	bitwise inversion

These are infix functions so we can call them without parentheses. This is how you'd shift by one bit to the right:

```
val n = 8 shr 1
```

Summary

In this chapter, we've seen how generics work and how Kotlin bypasses Java's type erasure with reified generics. We've also seen how Kotlin doesn't have any constructs for concurrent programming; instead, it leaves this to libraries. Then, we learned how Kotlin has another use for the by keyword with delegated properties. And, we covered Kotlin's DSL building features, and the receiver and infix functions. Finally, we explored how Kotlin supports operator overloading.

In the next chapter, we'll be exploring the *Kotlin Standard Library*. We'll learn about Collection types and see how Collections have numerous extension functions that work with function types. We'll also cover the most used and most helpful functions and extension functions.

6
Kotlin Standard Library

The Kotlin standard library is another feature of the language that makes it nicer to use in the daily programmer life. The library builds heavily on the Java standard library, in fact, it doesn't add many new types, rather, it adds new functionality with functions. It offers extensions functions that extend the Java standard library types or utility functions that can be used with any type.

We've already seen a lot of types and functions from the standard library (arrays, basic types, and more), and, in this chapter, we'll first learn about collections and see the most useful functions for working with collections. Then we'll take a look at the standard library functions.

In this chapter we will cover these topics :

- Collections
- Working with collections
- Kotlin standard library functions

Collections

Kotlin collections were inspired by Scala and its mutable and immutable collection types. Kotlin defines its collection types in the `kotlin.collections` package, and there you'll see that it basically redefines types that already exist in Java. But all of them get compiled to the Java version of the same type. So you don't have to worry that there is an additional overhead when using them.

The `Iterable` interface is the basis for all collection types. It has only one method, `iterator`, which returns an object that can iterate over a collection:

```
public interface Iterable<out T> {
    public operator fun iterator(): Iterator<T>
}
```

The `Iterator` object knows how to iterate over a collection. It has two methods: `next` which returns the next element, and `hasNext` which tells us if there any more elements in the collection:

```
public interface Iterator<out T>
{
    public operator fun next(): T
    public operator fun hasNext(): Boolean
}
```

The next interface in the hierarchy is the `Collection`. It adds a couple more functions to the `Iterable` interfaces, like the size of a collection, and a way to check if an element is contained inside a collection:

```
public interface Collection<out E> : Iterable<E> {
    public val size: Int
    public fun isEmpty(): Boolean
    public operator fun contains(element: @UnsafeVariance E): Boolean
    override fun iterator(): Iterator<E>
    public fun containsAll(elements: Collection<@UnsafeVariance E>):
Boolean
}
```

The next in the interface hierarchy are `List` and `Set`. They both extend the `Collection` interface. The `List` is an indexed collection, and with its `get` method, you can obtain an element from a collection by its position:

```
public interface List<out E> : Collection<E> {
    override val size: Int

    override fun isEmpty(): Boolean
    override fun contains(element: @UnsafeVariance E): Boolean
    override fun iterator(): Iterator<E>

    override fun containsAll(elements: Collection<@UnsafeVariance E>):
Boolean

    public operator fun get(index: Int): E

    public fun indexOf(element: @UnsafeVariance E): Int

    public fun lastIndexOf(element: @UnsafeVariance E): Int

    public fun listIterator(): ListIterator<E>

    public fun listIterator(index: Int): ListIterator<E>
```

```
        public fun subList(fromIndex: Int, toIndex: Int): List<E>
    }
```

The Set is an unindexed collection of unique elements, as can be seen in the following command:

```
public interface Set<out E> : Collection<E> {
    override val size: Int

    override fun isEmpty(): Boolean
    override fun contains(element: @UnsafeVariance E): Boolean
    override fun iterator(): Iterator<E>

    override fun containsAll(elements: Collection<@UnsafeVariance E>):
Boolean
}
```

There is also the Map interface which represents a collection of key-value pairs. The Map doesn't extend the Collection and Iterable interfaces:

```
public interface Map<K, out V> {
    public val size: Int

    public fun isEmpty(): Boolean

    public fun containsKey(key: K): Boolean

    public fun containsValue(value: @UnsafeVariance V): Boolean

    public operator fun get(key: K): V?

    @SinceKotlin("1.1")
    @PlatformDependent
    public fun getOrDefault(key: K, defaultValue: @UnsafeVariance V): V {
        return null as V
    }

    public val keys: Set<K>

    public val values: Collection<V>

    public val entries: Set<Map.Entry<K, V>>

    public interface Entry<out K, out V> {
        public val key: K
        public val value: V
    }
}
```

Now, all of these interfaces are present in Java, in the `java.util` package. But there is one big difference though: in Kotlin they are all read-only, that is, they are immutable. Kotlin differentiates between mutable and immutable collections. Each of these interfaces in Kotlin also has a mutable version, including the `MutableIterator` and `MutableList`.

The following table represents the Mutable and Immutable types with its Java representation:

Java Type	Kotlin Immutable Type	Kotlin Mutable Type
Iterable<E>	Iterable<E>	MutableIterable<E>
Collection<E>	Collection<E>	MutableCollection<E>
List<E>	List<E>	MutableList<E>
Set<E>	Set<E>	MutableSet<E>
Map<K, V>	Map<K, V>	MutableMap<K, V>

The mutable interfaces extend the immutable ones and add the methods for modifying the collections. Mutable versions are considered equal to their Java counterpart.

Types that you'll be working with mostly implement the `List`, `Set`, or `Map` interfaces and now we'll explore them in greater detail.

Lists

Lists are collections of indexed items. Lists support insertion and retrieval of items by their position. Besides the `ArrayList`class, which is probably the most used implementation, the `List` interface is also implemented in the `LinkedList` class. The `ArrayList` class is usually the one you'll use because it offers retrieval of items by position in constant time, and doesn't have the memory overhead of an additional `Node` object for each item which the LinkedList has. The Kotlin library provides several methods for creating instances of List interfaces. You can create the immutable instance of a List by calling the `listOf` function. The function accepts a `vararg` parameter which can be used to initialize the list with items:

```
val superHeros = listOf("Batman", "Superman", "Hulk")
```

There is also the `arrayListOf` function:

```
val moreSuperHeros = arrayListOf("Captain America", "Spider-Man")
```

If you are looking at the implementation of these methods, you might think that they are redundant, since both of them return an instance of the ArrayList class. The classes have the same name, but slightly different implementation. The one returned from the `listOf` function is a private class defined in the java.util.Arrays package. This is the same one you would get if you called the `Arrays.asList` function in Java. The `arrayListOf` function returns the "real" ArrayList class from the java.util package.

If you want to construct a mutable version of a List, there is the `mutableListOf` function:

```
val superHeros = mutableListOf("Thor", "Daredevil", "Iron Man")
```

This one can be modified as follows where the `add` method is defined in this version:

```
superHeros.add("Wolverine")
```

There is also the `emptyList` method which returns a read-only list with no items:

```
val empty = emptyList<String>()
```

Sets

A Set is a collection of unique elements. Sets have no ordering guarantees, so you cannot obtain an item by its position. There are several implementations of the Set interface in the Java standard library. Probably the most used one is the HashSet class. It can add, remove and check if an item is contained in a constant time. The LinkedHashSet class has roughly the same performance, but internally it uses a LinkedList for storing items. This comes with the added memory overhead of an additional Node object for each item it contains, but has the benefit of predictable iteration order. When the HashSet class is iterated, it is in an unspecified order, in other words, not in the order the items were inserted. There is also the TreeSet class, which orders its items based on their natural ordering (or by the order you specify with the Comparable interface). It stores its item inside a binary tree and this gives the TreeSet a slightly worse performance than the other two implementations(logarithmic instead of constant) for adding, getting, and checking whether an item is contained.

Constructing sets can be done by calling any of the previously mentioned implementations or using the functions from the standard library. Here are a couple of examples of immutable sets:

```
val superHeros = setOf("Batman", "Superman")
val superHeros2 = hashSetOf("Thor", "Spider-Man")
val superHeros3 = linkedSetOf("Iron-Man", "Wolverine")
val sortedNums = sortedSetOf(3,10,12,4,9)
val empty = emptySet<String>()
```

If you need a mutable set, there is only one function, mutableSetOf:

```
val mutableSet = mutableSetOf("Hulk", "DareDevil")
```

Maps

Maps are collections that associate keys to values. They have similar implementations to Sets. There is the most common HashMap class, an implementation that preserves insertion order when iterating; the LinkedHashMap; and the sorted version, the TreeMap. The performance of these classes is the same as with their Sets siblings. The Kotlin standard library has these functions for initializing immutable maps:

```
val map = mapOf(1 to "one", 2 to "two")
val hashMap = hashMapOf(3 to "three", 4 to "four")
val linkedMap = linkedMapOf(5 to "five", 6 to "six")
val sortedMap = sortedMapOf(7 to "seven", 8 to "eight")
val empty = emptyMap<Int, String>()
```

All these functions accept variable arguments of a Pair type to initialize the maps. We used the to extension function to create Pairs. This is the function in the standard library:

```
/**
 * Creates a tuple of type [Pair] from this and [that].
 *
 * This can be useful for creating [Map] literals with less noise, for
example:
 * @sample samples.collections.Maps.Instantiation.mapFromPairs
 */
public infix fun <A, B> A.to(that: B): Pair<A, B> = Pair(this, that)
```

It's an infix function, so we can call it without the parentheses.

For constructing a mutable map, there is only one function available, the mutableMapOf:

```
val mutableMap = mutableMapOf(9 to "nine", 10 to "ten")
```

Indexing

Lists and Maps have an option to get or set an item with the indexing operator, just as you can do with the arrays. Here's how you would get an item from the first position of a list:

```
val superHeros = mutableListOf("Superman", "Batman")
val superman = superHeros[0]
```

And this is how you would set an item at a certain position:

```
superHeros[2] = "Thor"
```

In the case of maps, you provide the key in the square brackets and the corresponding value is returned:

```
val map = mutableMapOf(1 to "one", 2 to "two")
val two = map[2]
```

And if you want to insert something into a map, you can put the key in the square brackets and then assign a value to that key:

```
map[3] = "three"
```

Platform types and immutable collections

Kotlin features like null safety are enforced during compile time and Kotlin tries to have (great) interoperability with Java. When Java code calls your Kotlin code it is already compiled and the Kotlin compiler cannot enforce its null checks. This is the reason why the Kotlin development team introduced a concept of a Platform Type. Simply put, a Platform Type is a type defined in Java (or any other JVM language).

In the case of nullability, Kotlin code can handle them as either nullable or non-nullable. If during runtime a null value is passed to a non-nullable variable, the Kotlin runtime will throw a null pointer exception.

Immutable Kotlin Collection types are treated similarly. Remember, Kotlin doesn't define its own Collection type, instead it uses the ones from Java. Since Java doesn't have the same concept of mutable and immutable collections (Java has immutable collections with specific types, such as the UnmodifiableList) it is up to the Kotlin code to treat them as mutable or immutable. This is not something you usually need to worry about.

But if you are communicating in the other direction, i.e. calling Java from Kotlin, then you have to be a bit more careful. Take a look at the following Java function:

```
public void checkStrings(List<String> strings) {
    for (String s : strings) {
        // do something
    }
    strings.add("Item added in Java");
}
```

We can imagine it does some string processing or validation and then it appends an item to the list. And we can pass an immutable list from Kotlin to it, as follows:

```
val strings = listOf("Item added in Kotlin", "Another item added in
Kotlin")
// UnsupportedOperationException thrown here
java.checkStrings(strings)
```

But calling this Java function will throw an UnsupportedOperationException during runtime. The reason is that the listOf function creates a specific implementation of the List interface, one that extends the AbstractList class and doesn't override the add method from it. The base implementation of the AbstractList add method just throws the UnsupportedOperationException. In cases like this, where you know that Java code is mutating a collection, always pass some version of a mutable version from Kotlin.

Now that you know how Kotlin Collection types use the corresponding Java types, and how Kotlin enforces collections immutability during compile time, it is easy to trick the compiler and modify the immutable collection with a simple cast. Consider this example where we declare an immutable list variable, assign to it an instance of the ArrayList class and then with a simple cast we are able to add more items to it:

```
val list: List<String> = ArrayList()
val mutableList = (list as ArrayList).add("string")
```

Finally, in the same way as with mutable and immutable properties, you should favor immutable collections. This can make your code have clearer intentions. For example, if you accept an immutable list as your parameter, then a user of your API knows that you are not modifying the collection with your code.

Working with collections

The standard library in the kotlin.collections package offers numerous extension functions that extend the collections types. Most of them extend the base Iterable interface, so they can be used with any collection type.

The library is too big to cover every function, so we'll see here the most useful ones. We can group them based on their operation.

Filtering functions

These functions are used to remove or filter items from a collection.

Drop

Drop removes first n elements from the collection.

```
val numbers = listOf(1, 2, 3, 4, 5)
val dropped = numbers.drop(2)
```

The `dropped` list now contains [3, 4, 5].

Filter

Filter applies the supplied predicate function to the collection and returns the following result:

```
val numbers = listOf(1, 2, 3, 4, 5)
val smallerThan3 = numbers.filter { n -> n < 3 }
```

The resulting list has these numbers [1, 2].

FilterNot

This is the inverted filter function:

```
val numbers = listOf(1, 2, 3, 4, 5)
val largerThan3 = numbers.filterNot { n -> n < 3 }
```

The resulting list has [4, 5].

Take

Take is the opposite of the `drop` function. It takes the first n elements from the collection:

```
val numbers = listOf(1, 2, 3, 4, 5)
val first2 = numbers.take(2)
```

The `first2` list now has [1, 2].

General functions

General functions are commonly used utility functions.

Any

Any returns true if the supplied predicate function matches any of the collection items:

```
val numbers = listOf(1, 2, 3, 4, 5)
val hasEvens = numbers.any { n -> n % 2 == 0 }
```

Any would return true in this case, as the predicate matches two items.

All

All is similar to any, but returns true if all the elements in the collection match the given predicate:

```
val numbers = listOf(1, 2, 3, 4, 5)
val allEven = numbers.all { n -> n % 2 == 0 }
```

It returns false in this case because not all numbers are even.

Count

Count returns the count of items that match the given predicate function:

```
val numbers = listOf(1, 2, 3, 4, 5)
val evenCount = numbers.count { n -> n % 2 == 0 }
```

In this case, number 2 is returned because there are 2 even numbers.

ForEach

This iterates over the collection and calls the given action function on each item:

```
val numbers = listOf(1, 2, 3, 4, 5)
numbers.forEach { n -> println(n) }
```

Max

Max returns the largest number in the collection:

```
val numbers = listOf(1, 2, 3, 4, 5)
val max = numbers.max()
```

Min

The opposite of max, min returns the smallest number in the collection:

```
val numbers = listOf(1, 2, 3, 4, 5)
val min = numbers.min()
```

Sum

This returns the sum of all numbers in the collection:

```
val numbers = listOf(1, 2, 3, 4, 5)
val sum = numbers.sum()
```

Note that the min, max and sum functions can only be used on collections with number types.

Transforming functions

Transforming functions are functions that can be used for converting items to another type.

Map

This applies the given transform function on each item in the collection:

```
val numbers = listOf(1, 2, 3, 4, 5)
val strings = numbers.map { n -> n.toString() }
```

We used it here to transform int type to string type.

FlatMap

This is similar to map, but the transform function returns a collection instead of one item, and then the resulting collections are flattened to a single one:

```
val numbers = listOf(1, 2, 3, 4, 5)
val multiplesOf10 = numbers.flatMap { n -> listOf(n, n * 10) }
```

Now the resulting list looks like this [1, 10, 2, 20, 3, 30, 4, 40, 5, 50]

GroupBy

This groups the elements into a Key-Value Map. The Key is the result of the selector function, and the value is the list of all the elements that satisfy the selector function condition:

```
val strings = listOf("abc", "ade", "bce", "bef")
val groupped = strings.groupBy { s -> s[0] }
```

We grouped here by the first character of the string, and now the grouped map looks like this ["a" : ["abc", "ade"], "b" : ["bce", "bef"].

AssociateBy

This is similar to groupBy, but doesn't create a List of values in the resulting Map. Instead, the value is always a single element, and, if more than one element satisfies the selector function, the last one in the iteration wins:

```
val numbers = listOf(1, 2, 3, 4, 5)
val groupped = numbers.associateBy { n -> n.toString() }
```

In this case, the selector takes the string representation of a number as the key, so the resulting Map looks like this ["1": 1, "2":2, "3":3, "4":4, "5":5]

Items functions

These functions can be used for obtaining items from a collection.

Contains

This function checks if a single item is contained in the collection:

```
val numbers = listOf(1, 2, 3, 4, 5)
val contains10 = numbers.contains(10)
```

First

This function returns the first item that satisfies the given predicate function or throws NoSuchElementException if no item satisfies the predicate:

```
val numbers = listOf(1, 2, 3, 4, 5)
val firstEven = numbers.first { n -> n % 2 == 0 }
```

FirstOrNull

This function is the same as `first`, but if no item satisfies the predicate then null is returned instead of throwing an exception:

```
val numbers = listOf(1, 2, 3, 4, 5)
val firstLargerThan10 = numbers.firstOrNull { n -> n > 10 }
```

Last

The opposite of the `first` function, last returns the last item that satisfies the predicate or throws the NoSuchElementException:

```
val numbers = listOf(1, 2, 3, 4, 5)
val lastEven = numbers.last { n -> n % 2 == 0 }
```

LastOrNull

The opposite of `firstOrNull`, this function returns the last item that satisfies the predicate or null in case of no items matching the predicate:

```
val numbers = listOf(1, 2, 3, 4, 5)
val lastLargerThan10 = numbers.lastOrNull { n -> n > 10 }
```

Single

This function scans the entire collection and returns the item that satisfies the predicate. If no items or more than one item match the predicate, then it throws an Exception.

```
val numbers = listOf(1, 2, 3, 4, 5)
val number5 = numbers.single { n -> n > 4 }
```

SingleOrNull

This function does the same job as the single, but instead of throwing an exception returns null if no or more than 1 item matches the predicate.

```
val numbers = listOf(1, 2, 3, 4, 5)
val smallerThan1 = numbers.singleOrNull { n -> n < 1 }
```

Sorting functions

These are functions that are used for sorting collection items. The items being sorted have to implement the generic Comparable<T> interface. If they don't, then you have to provide an instance of it that tells these function how to sort the items.

Reversed

This function reverses the order of items inside the collection:

```
val numbers = listOf(1, 2, 3, 4, 5)
val reversed = numbers.reversed()
```

Sorted

This function sorts the collection by their natural sort order. It can only be called if the generic type parameter implements the Comparable<T> interface:

```
val numbers = listOf(2, 1, 5, 3, 4)
val sorted = numbers.sorted()
```

SortedDescending

This sorts the items in descending order. In the same way as the sort function, items have to implement the Comparable interface:

```
val numbers = listOf(2, 1, 5, 3, 4)
val sortedDesc = numbers.sortedDescending()
```

Finally, here is how you can chain these functions and modify some data by only applying functions to it. Imagine that we are given a random list of integers and we have to produce a sorted collection of numbers that are squares of even numbers, where the highest number should be less than 1000, and they should be represented as strings. Here's one way to do it:

```
val result: List<String> = numbers.filter { n -> n % 2 == 0 }
        .map { n -> n * n }
        .sorted()
        .takeWhile { n -> n < 1000 }
        .map { n -> n.toString() }
```

Most of the functions return an Iterable type as a result and the calls can be chained, thus enabling functional style programming.

Kotlin standard library functions

The library provides a lot of useful functions for easier usage of the language and common programming tasks. We'll explore the contracts (preconditions) functions and the so-called standard functions.

Contracts

In the base Kotlin package, you can find several functions that can be used for runtime checking of data. They can be used for defining preconditions in functions. If you ever coded in Java then you probably wrote a not null precondition, with checking that an argument passed to a method is not null. The following methods are available, check, checkNotNull, require, requireNotNull and error. Let's show some examples of them.

Check

This function accepts a boolean condition and if it evaluates to false it will throw an IllegalStateException:

```
check(str.length > 5) { "Minimum length is 5" }
```

CheckNotNull

This function accepts a nullable argument, and, if it is null, throws an IllegalStateException. Otherwise, it returns the same argument as a non-nullable type:

```
val strNoNull: String = checkNotNull(str)
  { "str argument can not be null" }
```

Require

Require differs from check only in the kind of exception it throws, which is an IllegalArgumentException instead of an IllegalStateException:

```
require(str.length > 5)
{ "Minimum length is 5" }
```

RequireNotNull

This is the same as with `checkNotNull`, but with the difference that it throws an instance of the IllegalArgumentException class:

```
val strNoNulls: String = requireNotNull(str)
  { "str argument can not be null" }
```

Error

This function is a shortcut for throwing an instance of an IllegalStateException class:

```
error("Something went wrong")
```

Standard functions

The standard functions are defined in the Standard.kt file and that's probably why they are given that name. They all work in similar ways but are intended for different purposes, so now we'll explore each one of them.

Apply

This function extends the generic T parameter with no constraints, which means that any Type declared in Kotlin can use it. It accepts a receiver function, and the receiver is the instance on which the apply function is called and then returns the same instance. Since you can access the instance of the object inside the apply function, you can use it for creating objects and initializing them in the same place:

```
var stringBuilder = StringBuilder().apply {
    appendln("I'm the first line of the String Builder")
}
```

Here we created an instance of the StringBuilder class and used the `apply` function to append the first line.

Let

The Let function also extends the generic T type parameter, but it accepts a normal function as an argument and returns the result of that function. It can be used to do something with an object and then return a different value:

```
val str: String = StringBuilder().let { sb ->
    sb.appendln("First Line")
    sb.appendln("Second Line")
    sb.appendln("Third Line")
    sb.toString()
}
```

The lambda passed to let will get one argument, and that is the instance from which the let function was called. In this case, the `sb` argument is the StringBuilder instance from which we called the let function.

With

This function can be used to call multiple functions of an object without specifying a receiver. The function accepts an object and a receiver function of the same type as the object:

```
val stringBuilder = StringBuilder()
with(stringBuilder) {
    appendln("First Line")
    appendln("Second Line")
    appendln("Third Line")
}
```

Because the lambda is a receiver function, inside the lambda we have access to the object that was passed as an argument. In this case, we call `appendln` and the object that receives this function call is the one we pass in as the first argument.

With this function we can also return a different value. In the previous example, we didn't have a return value. Here's a similar example, but here a string is used as the return type:

```
val str: String = with(StringBuilder()) {
    appendln("First Line")
    appendln("Second Line")
    appendln("Third Line")
    toString()
}
```

Use

The Use function extends the Closable interface and is similar to Java's try with resources. It takes a lambda function, executes it and then closes the resource. The resource will be closed even if your lambda throws an exception:

```
val inputStream = "Kotlin".byteInputStream()
inputStream.use { stream ->
    val scanner = Scanner(stream)
    if (scanner.hasNext()) scanner.next() else ""
}
```

In this example, we used the lambda to read the stream. After the lambda gets executed, the use function calls close on the stream resource. Even if your lambda fails, like the next example shows, the use function will catch the exception, close the resource and then re-throw the exception:

```
val inputStream = "Kotlin".byteInputStream()
inputStream.use { stream ->
    error("Reading streams is not supported")
}
```

Summary

One of the reasons for Kotlin's great usability is its standard library. It is packed with numerous useful functions and constructs that can make common programming tasks easier. We covered the most commonly used ones, but since the library is an open source, you can explore it in detail and learn more about it at the official Kotlin web page.

In the next chapter, we'll put to use everything we've learned so far and use Kotlin to create a dictionary desktop app with JavaFx as our UI kit.

7
Coding a Dictionary App with Kotlin

In this final chapter, we'll get to see how Kotlin is used in practice. We'll create a cross-platform desktop dictionary application. The app will be rather small, but still this will be enough to see commonly used Kotlin features in action.

Some of the Kotlin features that we'll see in this app are the following: companion objects, properties, data classes, extension functions, receiver functions, lambdas, classes and interfaces, and generic and inline functions.

In this chapter, we will cover the following topics:

- Project setup
- Developing the dictionary app

Project setup

First, we need to set up our IDE and our development project. To compile our Kotlin project, we'll use Gradle as our build tool.

App features

The main feature of our app will be a fast lookup of words. For this, we will store our definitions inside an SQLite database and use its full-text search feature.

For the most part, we'll be using types from the Java Standard library, except for the JDBC SQLite database driver (`https://github.com/xerial/sqlite-jdbc`) and the Jackson JSON deserializing library (`https://github.com/FasterXML/jackson`).

Since we want to provide a fast lookup of words, the UI can be kept simple. We'll have a search area where a user can enter a word they want to look up, and below that, we'll display the results inside a `ListView`.

Requirements

To write this app, there aren't many requirements. Except for Kotlin and Java, you should also have Gradle installed. You can use any IDE you wish, but again IntelliJ IDEA Community Edition is recommended, as it works great with Kotlin and is completely free.

Finally, the dictionary words we will be using are already included with the code files that you can download from `https://github.com/PacktPublishing/Kotlin-Quick-Start-Guide`. They are in JSON format, with terms and definitions as JSON key-value pairs. The dictionary is free to use thanks to project Gutenberg: `http://www.gutenberg.org/`.

JavaFx will be our GUI library. JavaFx is a successor to the Java Swing framework and with version 8, it's part of the Java SDK and JRE. There is no need for prior knowledge of JavaFx; although the library and its API are rather big, we'll be explaining the basics as we work on the UI part of the app.

Creating the Kotlin-Gradle project

IntelliJ IDEA offers an option to create a Kotlin project with Gradle as the build system. In the **New Project** window, just select Gradle on the left and tick the **Kotlin** checkbox on the right:

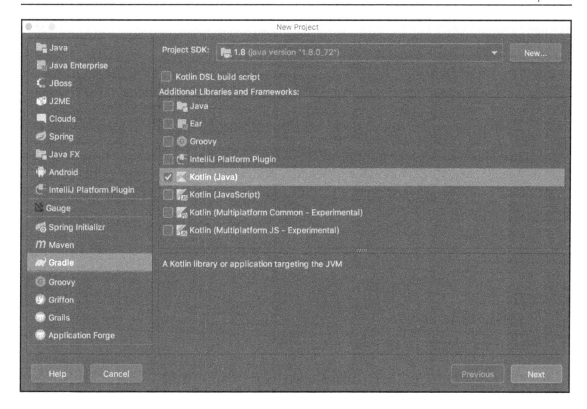

If you are using the downloaded code files, you can use the **New Project** from existing sources option to create an IntelliJ project (in the file selection dialog, just select the `build.gradle` file from the root of the source code folder).

With the project sorted out, next we need to set up our `build.gradle` file.

JavaFx apps are usually packaged with a tool called `javapackager`: `https://docs.oracle.com/javase/9/tools/javapackager.htm#JSWOR719`. There is a Gradle plugin for JavaFx (`https://github.com/FibreFoX/javafx-gradle-plugin`) that is a wrapper for this packager and enables assembling and distributing JavaFx apps with Gradle. This also enables running the project from IntelliJ with the click of a button.

IntelliJ created a `build.gradle` file for us. It should be located in the root of the project. Let's add the JavaFx plugin to the dependencies. Kotlin Gradle was added by IntelliJ, and below that we add the JavaFx plugin:

```
buildscript {
    ext.kotlin_version = '1.2.60'

    repositories {
        mavenCentral()
    }

    dependencies {
        classpath "org.jetbrains.kotlin:kotlin-gradle-
plugin:$kotlin_version"
        classpath group: 'de.dynamicfiles.projects.gradle.plugins', name:
'javafx-gradle-plugin', version: '8.8.2'
    }
}

group 'com.packt.kotlinquickstart'
version '1.0'
```

We also have to tell the Gradle to use it, and we apply it below the line to apply Kotlin:

```
apply plugin: 'kotlin'
apply plugin: 'javafx-gradle-plugin'
```

With the plugin added, we can configure the run configuration inside IntelliJ so we can run our app from the IDE. In the **Run** menu, click on the **Edit Configurations** menu option. Then, click on the + button in the upper-right corner and the **Add New Configuration** popup will appear. There, click on the **Gradle** option. Select our **English Dictionary** under the project and under **Tasks**, enter `jfxRun`:

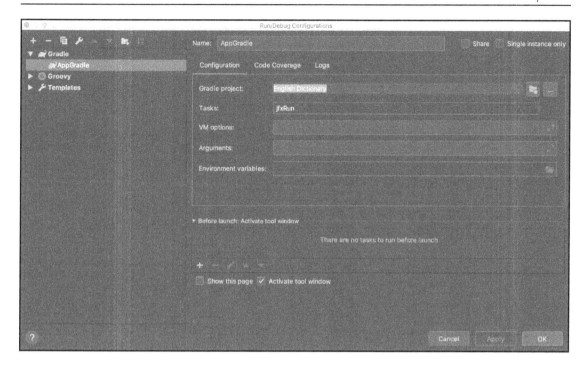

There is one more thing needed for the JavaFx plugin to work: we need to declare the main class of our JavaFx app. This class extends the JavaFx application class and it serves as the main entry point into our app.

Our package structure is com.packt.kotlinquickstart.dictionary, and this package structure is in the src/main/java folder. In that package, we'll now add the MainApp class:

```
class MainApp : Application()
```

The Application class has one abstract method, onStart, which we have to override:

```
public abstract void start(Stage primaryStage) throws Exception;
```

To make our code compile, we override it, but leave it empty for now:

```
override fun start(primaryStage: Stage) {
}
```

Back in the `build.gradle` file, we tell the JavaFx plugin to use this class as the entry point to our app:

```
jfx {
    mainClass = 'com.packt.kotlinquickstart.dictionary.MainApp'
    vendor = 'Packt Publishing'
}
```

Finally, in the dependencies section, we add the libraries we're going to use. We need the Kotlin Standard Library (compatible with Java 8), the JDBC driver for SQLite, and the Jackson JSON deserializer:

```
dependencies {
    compile 'org.jetbrains.kotlin:kotlin-stdlib-jre8:$kotlin_version'
    compile group: 'org.xerial', name: 'sqlite-jdbc', version: '3.21.0.1'
    compile group: 'com.fasterxml.jackson.core', name: 'jackson-databind',
version: '2.9.5'
}
```

Developing the dictionary app

With the IDE project, build tool, and required libraries sorted out, we can start developing our app.

Preparing the data

Since the dictionary words are stored in a JSON file, we need to parse the data before saving it to a local database.

First, we'll add the class that will represent our data. In the base package (`com.packt.quickstart.dictionary`), we first add a new package called `data`. There, we put the `DictionaryEntry` class, which will be our data model representation:

```
data class DictionaryEntry(val term: String, val explanation: String)
```

The class has two properties: the searchable term and the term definition. It'd be also nice to have a readable string representation of this class, so we let the Kotlin compiler generate a `toString` method for us with its data class.

Since the file of words is around 20 MB in size, to avoid loading that much data in the memory at once and deserializing the whole file in one go, we'll deserialize it manually, entry by entry.

For this, we'll build the `EntriesIterator` class, which can be iterated over, that is, it can supply dictionary entries one by one. That's why it implements the generic `Iterator` interface:

```
class EntriesIterator : Iterator<DictionaryEntry> {

    private val jsonParser: JsonParser = MappingJsonFactory()
.createParser(javaClass.classLoader.getResourceAsStream("dictionary.json"))
    private var currentToken: JsonToken?
```

`JsonParser` is the Jackson library class that provides an API for reading JSON content. We can get an instance of this class from the `MappingJsonFactory` type by providing an input stream. We've put the `dictionary.json` file in the project's resources folder. The easiest way to get an input stream of it is from the class loader that our classes are using.

In the class initializer (constructor), we obtain the current token of the JSON parser. The token represents the current location of a parser. Then, with a `while` loop, we position the token to the start of the first entry:

```
init {
    currentToken = jsonParser.currentToken
    while (currentToken != JsonToken.FIELD_NAME) {
        currentToken = jsonParser.nextToken()
    }
}
```

Our JSON file is structured like this:

```
{
    "exportable" : "Suitable for exportation; as, exportable products.",
    "irrisible" : "Not risible. [R.],
    ...
}
```

So, the first token will be `START_OBJECT` and the last one will be `LAST_OBJECT`. The dictionary term will be under `FIELD_NAME` and the definition will under the `VALUE_STRING` token.

With this information, we can implement the two required methods of the `Iterator` interface.

`hasNext` returns true until we reach the end object token:

```
override fun hasNext(): Boolean {
    return currentToken != JsonToken.END_OBJECT
}
```

And the `next` method has to return a `DictionaryEntry` instance. It does that by reading the JSON key-value pair from the JSON parser:

```
override fun next(): DictionaryEntry {
    var term = ""
    var definition = ""
    if (currentToken == JsonToken.FIELD_NAME) {
        term = jsonParser.valueAsString
        currentToken = jsonParser.nextToken()
    }

    if (currentToken == JsonToken.VALUE_STRING) {
        definition = jsonParser.valueAsString
        currentToken = jsonParser.nextToken()
    }

    if (currentToken == JsonToken.END_OBJECT) {
        jsonParser.close()
    }

    return DictionaryEntry(term, definition)
}
```

We also check whether we have reached the end of the JSON file so we can properly close the parser, which will close the input stream for us.

Now that we have a type that can parse the JSON file and create dictionary entries, we need to save them to a database.

The JDBC driver will need to establish a connection to our database and give us a `Connection` object if we wish to query or manipulate the database. We'll create a separate type that takes care of this. In the same package, let's add the `DbConnectionProvider` interface:

```
interface DbConnectionProvider {
    fun getConnection(): Connection

    companion object {
        val defaultProvider: DbConnectionProvider =
LocalDbConnectionProvider()
    }
}

private class LocalDbConnectionProvider : DbConnectionProvider {
    override fun getConnection(): Connection =
DriverManager.getConnection("jdbc:sqlite:dictionary.db")
}
```

Notice how Kotlin allows companion objects inside interfaces also. Our companion object holds the default implementation of the interface inside a property. The default implementation is defined in the same file and is hidden from outside, as the class is marked as private.

The database file will be in the same folder as our app, so construction of the connection URL is pretty simple; we just need the database filename after the `jdbc:sqlite` URL.

Next is the `DictionaryLoader` class, which will iterate over all entries and save them to a database. This is a long-running operation and it will be done asynchronously. Writing async code got a lot easier in Java 8, thanks to the `CompletableFuture` class. It implements the `Future` interface, which has been present in Java since version 1.5, but the problem with previous implementations of this interface was that calling its `get` function to obtain a result would block the calling thread until a result became available. Working with `CompletableFuture` is a lot nicer, since it offers triggering actions and invoking functions upon its completion. It even allows executing these functions on a different executor/thread. This makes it perfect for our use case; we can offload the long-running database loading to a background thread and then schedule a completion task on the main thread:

```
class DictionaryLoader(private val iterator: Iterator<DictionaryEntry>,
                       private val dbConnectionProvider:
DbConnectionProvider = DbConnectionProvider.defaultProvider) {

    fun loadDictionary(): CompletableFuture<Void> {
        return CompletableFuture.runAsync {
            dbConnectionProvider.getConnection().use { conn ->
                conn.prepareStatement("INSERT INTO entries(entry,
explanation) VALUES (?, ?)").use { stmnt ->
                    iterator.forEach { e ->
                        stmnt.setString(1, e.term)
                        stmnt.setString(2, e.explanation)
                        stmnt.executeUpdate()
                    }
                }
            }
        }
    }
}
```

The easiest way to create `CompletableFuture` is to call the static `runAsync` function and provide a lambda that will be executed asynchronously. We don't have to specify an `Executor` that will be used for this task; by default, a `ForkJoinPool` is used, which is more than enough for our case.

The `loadDictionary` function returns a generic `CompletableFuture`. The `Void` generic parameter says that there is no result in this `Future`. We could have also used Kotlin's `Unit`, but then the lambda should explicitly return a `Unit`. That is because when a `CompletableFuture` is built with a `Runnable`, `runAsync` returns `CompletableFuture<Void>`:

```
public static CompletableFuture<Void> runAsync(Runnable runnable)
```

Inside the lambda, we get a `Connection` object from our `DbConnectionProvider`. The `Connection` interface extends the `Closable` interface since database connections should be closed after we're done with them. We'll close them with the `use` function from the Kotlin Standard Library. Since we'll be inserting a lot of rows into the database, we can make the initial population faster if we precompile the SQL Insert statement. The `Connection` object has a method for it; `prepareStatement` takes an SQL command and returns a `PreparedStatement` object. Notice how we used two question marks in the SQL command; these are command parameters and we bind them to our model's term and explanation properties when we iterate the whole word list.

`PreparedStatement` is also closable, and again Kotlin's `use` function makes sure that it gets closed properly.

The last thing our data package needs is a repository type, which will talk to the database and offer a search function. Let's add the `Repository` class in the same package:

```
class Repository(private val dbConnectionProvider: DbConnectionProvider =
DbConnectionProvider.defaultProvider)
```

The `Repository` class also needs a connection, and it will also get it from `DbConnectionProvider`. We'll again be working with `Statements` and `PreparedStatements`. To make the code a bit nicer and shorter, and to also show how receiver functions can be used, first we'll write two helper functions. They will obtain a connection, create a statement, and then execute the receiver function on that statement. `prepareStatement` works with the `PreparedStatement` object:

```
private inline fun <T> prepareStatement(sql: String, block:
PreparedStatement.() -> T): T {
    dbConnectionProvider.getConnection().use { conn ->
        conn.prepareStatement(sql).use { stmt ->
            return stmt.block()
        }
    }
}
```

The function is generic as we want to have the option of returning different types from this helper function. Although this is not needed in our small app, the purpose is to show how Kotlin can be used. Also, we marked it `inline`, so the compiler will inline the receiver lambda directly to the call site.

The second one is similar but works with `Statement` objects:

```
private inline fun <T> executeStatement(block: Statement.() -> T): T {
    dbConnectionProvider.getConnection().use { conn ->
        conn.createStatement().use { stmt ->
            return stmt.block()
        }
    }
}
```

For searching dictionary entries, we'll need to extract data from a `ResultSet` object. `ResultSet` internally holds a cursor that points to a row in a database and is moved forward with its `next` function. We can create an extension function on `ResultSet` that knows how to extract all dictionary entries from it:

```
private fun ResultSet.getEntries(): List<DictionaryEntry> {
    val entries = ArrayList<DictionaryEntry>()
    while (this.next()) {
        val term = this.getString(1)
        val explanation = this.getString(2)
        entries.add(DictionaryEntry(term, explanation))
    }
    return entries
}
```

With these helper functions in place, our `search` function is only two lines of code:

```
fun search(searchTerm: String, exactMatch: Boolean = true):
List<DictionaryEntry> {
    return prepareStatement("SELECT * FROM entries WHERE entry MATCH ?") {
        setString(1, if (exactMatch) searchTerm else "$searchTerm*")
        executeQuery().use { resultSet -> resultSet.getEntries() }
    }
}
```

The `prepareStatement` function takes an SQL command and a receiver lambda. Inside the receiver lambda, we work with the `PreparedStatement` object of this SQL command, set the string parameter, execute it, and return the dictionary entries with our extension function.

We also need a method for creating our full-text search table. This method will be called each time our app starts, so we create the table only if it doesn't exist:

```
fun onStart() {
    executeStatement { executeUpdate("CREATE VIRTUAL TABLE IF NOT EXISTS
entries USING FTS4 (entry, explanation)") }
}
```

And finally, we need a function that will tell us if the data from the JSON file has been loaded. If the database is empty, our app will show a loading screen while we're parsing and inserting the data:

```
fun isDataLoaded(): Boolean {
    return executeStatement {
        val result = executeQuery("SELECT COUNT(*) FROM entries")
        result.next() && result.getInt(1) > 0
    }
}
```

Building the UI

Now that we have the data part of app sorted, we can start working on the UI. The app will have two screens, or scenes in JavaFx. The loading scene will be shown only when the app runs for the first time. It will show a progress indicator while we parse the JSON file and populate our database. The second scene will be the main part of our app where a user can search for words and terms.

Loading scene

With JavaFx, there are two ways of defining UI elements. One is using Kotlin (or Java) code to create UI control class instances and then styling them and positioning them programmatically. The other way is using FXML, which is an XML-based markup language.

With FXML, we can separate the presentation part of our app from the application logic part and that's why we'll use it for our UI.

FXML doesn't have a schema, it maps directly to JavaFx control classes. This means that you don't have to learn FXML, you can look into the JavaFx documentation and see what controls are available and what properties they offer. The full documentation of the API is available here: https://docs.oracle.com/javase/8/javafx/api/toc.htm.

Let's start with the loading screen. In the resources folder of our project, add a new file called `loader.fxml`. Here, we'll define our loading scene. The scene is pretty simple; we need two controls, a label to display that we're loading the data, and a progress indicator:

```
<?xml version="1.0" encoding="UTF-8"?>

<?import javafx.geometry.Insets?>
<?import javafx.scene.control.Label?>
<?import javafx.scene.control.ProgressIndicator?>
<?import javafx.scene.layout.VBox?>
<?import javafx.scene.text.Font?>

<VBox
fx:controller="com.packt.kotlinquickstart.dictionary.LoadingController"
        alignment="CENTER" maxHeight="-Infinity" maxWidth="-Infinity"
        minHeight="-Infinity" minWidth="-Infinity" prefHeight="400.0"
        prefWidth="600.0" xmlns="http://javafx.com/javafx/8.0.121"
        xmlns:fx="http://javafx.com/fxml/1">
    <Label alignment="CENTER" text="Loading Dictionary Data ..."
            textAlignment="JUSTIFY">
        <font>
            <Font name="Arial" size="19.0"/>
        </font>
        <VBox.margin>
            <Insets bottom="20.0"/>
        </VBox.margin>
    </Label>
    <ProgressIndicator>
        <opaqueInsets>
            <Insets bottom="10.0" left="10.0" right="10.0" top="10.0"/>
        </opaqueInsets>
    </ProgressIndicator>
</VBox>
```

At the top of the file, you can see how all the controls used in the file are first imported. The imports use the full class name, including the package name. If you know the name of the control you wish to use, you can start typing the name and IntelliJ will auto-complete and insert the import statement for you.

The root of our scene is a `VBox` control, which lays its children out inside a single vertical column. The root control also has the `fx:controller` attribute, which has a class that we don't have yet. This class will be our controller for this UI scene. Controllers can manage the UI and define the logic for our scene.

Now, back in the `MainApp` class, we'll add a function for changing scenes:

```
private fun changeScene(fxml: String, title: String = "Dictionary") {
    val page = FXMLLoader.load(javaClass.classLoader.getResource(fxml)) as
Parent
    var scene = stage.scene
    stage.title = title
    if (scene == null) {
        scene = Scene(page, 900.0, 700.0)
        stage.scene = scene
    } else {
        stage.scene.root = page
    }
    stage.sizeToScene()
}
```

The function accepts the name of an FXML file and optionally a title for the scene. The whole UI control hierarchy can be created from an FXML file with the load function call to the FXMLoader class. When the scene is loaded, it is placed as the root of the stage our app was created with.

While we are still in the `MainApp` class, we can add a function that our `LoadingController` will invoke when it is done loading the data. We will then navigate to the main scene:

```
fun onDictionaryLoaded() {
    changeScene("main.fxml")
}
```

We can also add the `main.fxml` file to the resources folder and leave it empty for now.

Our `LoadingController` will also need an instance of `MainApp` so it can invoke the `onDictionaryLoaded` function. We can add a `MainApp` property to the companion object:

```
companion object {
    lateinit var instance: MainApp
}
```

And then, add a constructor where we initialize this property:

```
init {
    instance = this
}
```

We have everything we need to finish the `MainApp` class. The `stage` property is the one that is provided by the JavaFx in the `start` function. We store it so we can change the scenes in the `changeScene` function:

```
private lateinit var stage: Stage
```

And finally, we have the `start` function:

```
override fun start(primaryStage: Stage) {
    stage = primaryStage

    val repository = Repository()
    repository.onStart()
    if (repository.isDataLoaded()) {
        changeScene("main.fxml")
    } else {
        changeScene("loader.fxml")
    }

    primaryStage.show()
}
```

We check we have loaded the data; if not, we navigate to the loader scene and if yes, we go straight to the main scene.

To finish the loading scene, we'll need to implement the controller class for it. But before we do that, we can create an implementation of the Java executor interface that schedules actions on the main thread of our JavaFx App. We'll use it on the `CompletableFuture` API, so we can schedule actions that interact with the UI on the main thread of our app. Executing a `Runnable` on the main JavaFx thread is done with the `Platform.runLater` method call:

```
class MainThreadExecutor private constructor() : Executor {

    override fun execute(command: Runnable) {
        Platform.runLater(command)
    }

    companion object {
        private val instance = MainThreadExecutor()

        val INSTANCE
            get() = instance
    }
}
```

We can get by with only one instance of this class, so we made it a singleton. A private constructor ensures that we can construct an instance from inside the class and we do that inside a companion object, which also exposes a public instance property.

Finally, there is the `LoadingController` implementation. An instance of this class will be created by JavaFx when the Loading scene gets initialized. That's why the class needs to have a parameterless constructor.

The logic of the controller is really simple: it has to load the data into the database and then notify `MainApp` when it is done. Here's the full code of the controller:

```
class LoadingController {

    private val loader = DictionaryLoader(EntriesIterator())

    @FXML
    fun initialize() {
        loader.loadDictionary()
                .thenRunAsync(Runnable {
    MainApp.instance.onDictionaryLoaded() }
                        , MainThreadExecutor.INSTANCE)
                .handle { _, fail -> if (fail != null) Platform.runLater {
    onError(fail) } }
    }

    private fun onError(fail: Throwable) {
        val alert = Alert(Alert.AlertType.ERROR)
        alert.headerText = "An error occurred!"
        alert.dialogPane.expandableContent =
    ScrollPane(TextArea(fail.message))
        alert.showAndWait()
    }
}
```

If you define a function called `initialize` and apply the FXML annotation to it, then JavaFx will invoke it when it has finished loading all the UI controls. In our case, we start loading dictionary data into that function.

The `loadDicationary` function returns `CompletableFuture`. We want to notify `MainApp` we are done loading the dictionary, so we schedule a completion action for this `CompletableFuture` with a `thenRunAsync` call. We schedule it on the main thread of our app with the `MainThreadExecutor` we created in the previous section.

If something goes wrong while we're loading the data, we want to notify the user about it. That's why added the `handle` function call, which will be invoked if an exception is thrown.

If we now run the app, you should see our loading scene while the dictionary database is being populated:

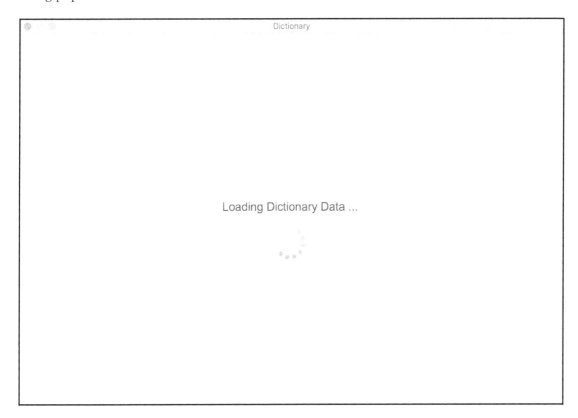

Main Scene

With the database loaded, we can now build the main UI part of our app. The Main Scene will have a search area on the top, and below we'll display the results of a search. The results will be displayed inside a `ListView` control, which is a scrollable list of items.

ListView displays its items as ListCell controls. ListCell is a generic type, where the generic parameter represents the item ListView is rendering. In our case, this is the DictionaryEntry type. Since we want to tell ListView how to render our DictionaryEntry type, we'll create our own DictionaryEntryCell type that extends ListCell and overrides its updateItem method. First, we'll add a new FXML file to the resources folder. dictionary_entry_cell.fxml represents the UI part of our custom ListCell:

```xml
<?xml version="1.0" encoding="UTF-8"?>

<?import javafx.geometry.Insets?>
<?import javafx.scene.control.Label?>
<?import javafx.scene.layout.VBox?>
<?import javafx.scene.text.Font?>

<VBox fx:id="cellHost" maxHeight="Infinity" minWidth="40" prefWidth="100.0"
        xmlns="http://javafx.com/javafx/8.0.121"
        xmlns:fx="http://javafx.com/fxml/1">
    <VBox.margin>
        <Insets top="10.0"/>
    </VBox.margin>

    <Label fx:id="termLbl" lineSpacing="3.0">
        <VBox.margin>
            <Insets top="5.0"/>
        </VBox.margin>
        <font>
            <Font name="System Bold" size="22.0"/>
        </font>
    </Label>

    <Label fx:id="explanationLbl" lineSpacing="1.0" minWidth="200.0"
            text="Definition" textAlignment="JUSTIFY" textFill="#6f6f6f">
        <VBox.margin>
            <Insets left="8.0" top="8.0"/>
        </VBox.margin>
        <font>
            <Font name="Arial" size="12.0"/>
        </font>
    </Label>
    <padding>
        <Insets bottom="4.0" left="16.0" right="12.0" top="8.0"/>
    </padding>

</VBox>
```

The cell has two label controls, stacked one above the other inside a VBox. Notice how these controls have the `fx:id` attribute. This allows us to reference these controls inside a controller. When JavaFx instantiates a controller, it will scan all fields (or properties in Kotlin) that have the FXML annotation, and if the field type matches the JavaFx Control type and the name equals the `fx:id` attribute, it will assign that control to that field. This will be needed, because we'll be setting the text property of these labels dynamically, based on the `DictionaryEntry` object's data.

Now, we can create a class that will load this FXML file:

```
class DictionaryEntryCell: ListCell<DictionaryEntry>() {

    @FXML
    private lateinit var termLbl: Label

    @FXML
    private lateinit var explanationLbl: Label

    @FXML
    private lateinit var cellHost: VBox

    init {
        val fxmlLoader =
FXMLLoader(javaClass.classLoader.getResource("dictionary_entry_cell.fxml"))
        fxmlLoader.setController(this)
        fxmlLoader.load<DictionaryEntryCell>()
    }

    @FXML
    fun initialize() {
        explanationLbl.isWrapText = true
        explanationLbl.textAlignment = TextAlignment.JUSTIFY
    }

    override fun updateItem(dictionaryEntry: DictionaryEntry?, empty:
Boolean) {
        super.updateItem(item, empty)
        if (dictionaryEntry != null && !empty) {
            termLbl.text = dictionaryEntry.term
            explanationLbl.text = dictionaryEntry.explanation
            graphic = cellHost
        } else {
            graphic = null
            text = ""
        }
    }
}
```

You can see how the FXML annotated properties have the same name as the
`fx:id` attribute in the FXML file. They are `lateinit` because they will be set after the class
constructor gets called. The initialize method will be called after all FXML properties are
set, so it is safe to access them inside this method.

In the class constructor, we load our FXML file. Controllers can also be set
programmatically, as you can see, with the `setController` method call.

The most important thing is the `updateItem` method; it gets called by the `ListView` when
it wants to render our `DictionaryEntry`. It is also called when an item gets removed, so
before setting the text values on the labels, we check that the entry is not empty.

Now, we can finally start with the main scene of our app. First, we'll add the
`main.fxml` file to the resources folder:

```xml
<?xml version="1.0" encoding="UTF-8"?>

<?import javafx.geometry.Insets?>
<?import javafx.scene.Cursor?>
<?import javafx.scene.control.Button?>
<?import javafx.scene.control.CheckBox?>
<?import javafx.scene.control.Label?>
<?import javafx.scene.control.TextArea?>
<?import javafx.scene.layout.HBox?>
<?import javafx.scene.layout.StackPane?>
<?import javafx.scene.layout.VBox?>

<VBox fx:id="root" maxHeight="-Infinity" maxWidth="-Infinity"
      minHeight="-Infinity" minWidth="-Infinity" prefHeight="400.0"
      prefWidth="600.0" xmlns="http://javafx.com/javafx/8.0.121"
      xmlns:fx="http://javafx.com/fxml/1"
      fx:controller="com.packt.kotlinquickstart.dictionary.MainController">
   <HBox alignment="TOP_CENTER" maxHeight="75.0" minHeight="50.0"
         prefHeight="50.0" prefWidth="200.0"
StackPane.alignment="TOP_CENTER">
      <TextArea fx:id="searchText" maxHeight="30.0" minHeight="20.0"
                prefHeight="20.0" prefWidth="200.0" promptText="sarch
term">
         <HBox.margin>
            <Insets bottom="10.0" right="20.0" top="10.0"/>
         </HBox.margin>
         <cursor>
            <Cursor fx:constant="TEXT"/>
         </cursor>
      </TextArea>
      <Button id="searchBtn" fx:id="searchBtn"
alignment="BASELINE_CENTER"
```

```
                contentDisplay="CENTER" minHeight="20.0"
  mnemonicParsing="false"
                prefHeight="30.0" text="Search">
            <HBox.margin>
                <Insets top="10.0"/>
            </HBox.margin>
        </Button>
        <CheckBox fx:id="exactMatchCb" text="Exact match">
            <HBox.margin>
                <Insets left="40.0" top="15.0"/>
            </HBox.margin>
        </CheckBox>
    </HBox>
    <Label fx:id="noResultsText" managed="false" maxHeight="-Infinity"
        prefHeight="30.0" text="No results matching the search"
        VBox.vgrow="NEVER">
        <VBox.margin>
            <Insets bottom="10.0" left="20.0" top="10.0"/>
        </VBox.margin>
    </Label>
</VBox>
```

Again, nothing special about the UI part. We use VBoxes for vertical stacking and HBoxes for the horizontal stacking of child controls. We haven't defined the ListView control in the FXML; we'll be creating it in Kotlin code. There were some problems with clearing items from the ListView; sometimes, when setting new search results and new items for the ListView, it displayed items from the previous search results. To avoid this, each search will get a new instance of the ListView class.

The FXML file already has the fx:controller attribute; now we'll create this final class of our app. The MainController class will be responsible for taking the search input and querying the database for results. First, let's add all the FXML controls we defined in the FXML file:

```
class MainController {

    @FXML
    private lateinit var root: VBox

    @FXML
    private lateinit var searchBtn: Button

    @FXML
    private lateinit var searchText: TextArea

    @FXML
```

```
        private lateinit var exactMatchCb: CheckBox

    @FXML
        private lateinit var noResultsText: Label

        private var listView: ListView<DictionaryEntry>? = null
```

The `ListView` property doesn't have the FXML annotation, as it is not defined in FXML. Other properties will be set by JavaFx, when it creates an instance of this controller class.

We'll also need a Repository instance and an instance of a generic `ObservableList` interface:

```
    private val repository = Repository()
    private val observableItems =
    FXCollections.observableArrayList<DictionaryEntry>()
```

The `ListView` constructor accepts an `ObservableList` object and this is the one we'll use for storing our search results.

We'll also need two helper functions, which will be used for recreating the `Listview`:

```
    private fun clearListView()
    {
        root.children.removeAll(listView)
        observableItems.clear()
        createListView()
    }

    private fun createListView()
    {
        listView = ListView(observableItems)
        listView.cellFactory = Callback { DictionaryEntryCell() }
        root.children.add(listView)
        VBox.setVgrow(listView, Priority.ALWAYS)
    }
```

Triggering a search can be done with a click on the search button or by pressing the *Enter* key in the text area. In both cases, we'll respond to the appropriate event so we need to define event handlers for these two controls:

```
    @FXML
    fun initialize()
    {
        searchBtn.onMouseClicked = EventHandler
            {
```

```
            onSearchClicked()

    }

        searchText.onKeyPressed = EventHandler { event ->
            if (event.code == KeyCode.ENTER) {
                event.consume()
                onSearchClicked()
            }
        }

        createListView()
    }
```

Finally, here is the onSearchClicked function:

```
    private fun onSearchClicked()
    {
        noResultsText.isManaged = false
        clearListView()

        val text = searchText.text?.trim()
        if (text != null && text.isNotEmpty())
        {
            CompletableFuture.supplyAsync
            {
                repository.search(text, exactMatchCb.isSelected)
            }.thenAcceptAsync(Consumer { results ->
                if (results.isNotEmpty())
                {
                    observableItems.addAll(results)
                } else {
                    noResultsText.isManaged = true
                }
            }, MainThreadExecutor.INSTANCE)
        }
    }
```

Before querying the database, we hide the noResultsText control and recreate listView. Since we are interested in the result of CompletableFuture, we create it with the supplyAsync call. This enables us to get the results with the thenAcceptAsync function call, which is scheduled on the main thread because it will interact with our UI controls. When we have the results, we add them to the observableItems object. Since ObservableList knows when items change, ListView will render the new items automatically. And if the results are empty, we just show noResultsText.

We can now run the app, and if the database has been loaded, we'll enter the main screen of our app where we can search for words and definitions:

Summary

In this final chapter, we've built an app step by step. Although the app we wrote wasn't big, it gave us enough room to see Kotlin features in action.

Most of the types we used were from the Java Standard Library or written in Java itself. This showed how good the interoperability with Java and existing Java types is.

We've also seen how Kotlin works with a popular build tool such as Gradle, and how it has first-class support in IntelliJ IDE.

After this final chapter, where we showed how Kotlin is used in practice, you should have a good understanding of the language and its features.

Other Books You May Enjoy

If you enjoyed this book, you may be interested in these other books by Packt:

Kotlin Programming By Example
Iyanu Adelekan

ISBN: 978-1-78847-454-2

- Learn the building blocks of the Kotlin programming language
- Develop powerful RESTful microservices for Android applications
- Create reactive Android applications efficiently
- Implement an MVC architecture pattern and dependency management using Kotlin
- Centralize, transform, and stash data with Logstash
- Secure applications using Spring Security
- Deploy Kotlin microservices to AWS and Android applications to the Play Store

Kotlin Programming Cookbook
Aanand Shekhar Roy, Rashi Karanpuria

ISBN: 978-1-78847-214-2

- Understand the basics and object-oriented concepts of Kotlin Programming
- Explore the full potential of collection frameworks in Kotlin
- Work with SQLite databases in Android, make network calls, and fetch data over a network
- Use Kotlin's Anko library for efficient and quick Android development
- Uncover some of the best features of Kotlin: Lambdas and Delegates
- Set up web service development environments, write servlets, and build RESTful services with Kotlin
- Learn how to write unit tests, integration tests, and instrumentation/acceptance tests.

Leave a review - let other readers know what you think

Please share your thoughts on this book with others by leaving a review on the site that you bought it from. If you purchased the book from Amazon, please leave us an honest review on this book's Amazon page. This is vital so that other potential readers can see and use your unbiased opinion to make purchasing decisions, we can understand what our customers think about our products, and our authors can see your feedback on the title that they have worked with Packt to create. It will only take a few minutes of your time, but is valuable to other potential customers, our authors, and Packt. Thank you!

Index

operator overloading
  about 107, 108
  bitwise operations 110
  with extension functions 109
  with Java 109
overriding 52, 53

P

packages 34, 35
primary constructors 42, 43
primitive types 21
properties 39, 40, 41

R

receiver functions 103, 104
reference types 21
reified generics 94

S

safe casting 28
SAM types 81, 82
sealed classes 66, 67
secondary constructors 43, 44
Sets 115
Single Abstract Method 81
singletons
  creating, with object keyword 58, 59, 60
smart casts 67, 68
sorting functions, collections
  about 124
  reversed 124
  sorted 124
  SortedDescending 124
standard functions
  about 126
  apply 127
  let 127

use 128
  with 127
standard library delegate properties
  about 99
  lazy 99
  notNull 101
  observable 100
  vetoable 100
standard library functions
  about 125
  contracts 125
  standard functions 126
static keyword
  with companion objects 62
strings 24
synchronized keyword 96

T

transforming functions, collections
  about 121
  AssociateBy 122
  FlatMap 121
  GroupBy 122
  map 121
type erasure 93
type inference 21

U

upper bound constraint 92

V

variable function arguments 73
visibility modifiers 35, 36
volatile keyword 97

W

while loops 32